Cambridge Elements

Elements in Language, Gender and Sexuality
edited by
Helen Sauntson
York St John University

PRIDE IN ASIA

Negotiating Ideologies, Localness, and Alternative Futures

Benedict J. L. Rowlett
Hong Kong Baptist University

Pavadee Saisuwan
Chulalongkorn University

Christian Go
University of the Philippines

Li-Chi Chen
Kazimierz Wielki University

Mie Hiramoto
National University of Singapore

Shaftesbury Road, Cambridge CB2 8EA, United Kingdom

One Liberty Plaza, 20th Floor, New York, NY 10006, USA

477 Williamstown Road, Port Melbourne, VIC 3207, Australia

314–321, 3rd Floor, Plot 3, Splendor Forum, Jasola District Centre, New Delhi – 110025, India

103 Penang Road, #05–06/07, Visioncrest Commercial, Singapore 238467

Cambridge University Press is part of Cambridge University Press & Assessment, a department of the University of Cambridge.

We share the University's mission to contribute to society through the pursuit of education, learning and research at the highest international levels of excellence.

www.cambridge.org
Information on this title: www.cambridge.org/9781009565370

DOI: 10.1017/9781009415804

© Benedict J. L. Rowlett, Pavadee Saisuwan, Christian Go, Li-Chi Chen, and Mie Hiramoto 2025

This publication is in copyright. Subject to statutory exception and to the provisions of relevant collective licensing agreements, no reproduction of any part may take place without the written permission of Cambridge University Press & Assessment.

When citing this work, please include a reference to the DOI 10.1017/9781009415804

First published 2025

A catalogue record for this publication is available from the British Library

ISBN 978-1-009-56537-0 Hardback
ISBN 978-1-009-41579-8 Paperback
ISSN 2634-8772 (online)
ISSN 2634-8764 (print)

Cambridge University Press & Assessment has no responsibility for the persistence or accuracy of URLs for external or third-party internet websites referred to in this publication and does not guarantee that any content on such websites is, or will remain, accurate or appropriate.

Pride in Asia

Negotiating Ideologies, Localness, and Alternative Futures

Elements in Language, Gender and Sexuality

DOI: 10.1017/9781009415804
First published online: January 2025

Benedict J. L. Rowlett
Hong Kong Baptist University

Pavadee Saisuwan
Chulalongkorn University

Christian Go
University of the Philippines

Li-Chi Chen
Kazimierz Wielki University

Mie Hiramoto
National University of Singapore

Author for correspondence: Benedict J. L. Rowlett, browlett@hkbu.edu.hk

Abstract: This Element provides a transregional overview of Pride in Asia, exploring the multifaceted nature of Pride in contemporary LGBTQIA+ events in Thailand, the Philippines, Taiwan, and Hong Kong. This collaborative research that combines individual studies draws on linguistic landscapes as an analytical and methodological approach. Each section examines the different manifestations of Pride as a discourse and the affordances and limitations of this discourse in facilitating the social, political, and cultural projects of LGBTQIA+ people in Asia, illustrating both commonalities and specificities in Asian Pride movements. Analyzing a variety of materials such as protest signs, t-shirts, and media reports, each section illustrates how modes of semiosis, through practice, intersect notions of gender and sexuality with broader social and political formations. The authors thus emphasize the need to view Pride not as a uniform global phenomenon but as a dynamic, locally shaped expression of LGBTQIA+ solidarity.

This Element also has a video abstract: www.cambridge.org/ELGS_Rowlett

Keywords: LGBTQIA+, Pride, Asia, linguistic landscapes, discourse analysis.

© Benedict J. L. Rowlett, Pavadee Saisuwan, Christian Go, Li-Chi Chen, and Mie Hiramoto 2025

ISBNs: 9781009565370 (HB), 9781009415798 (PB), 9781009415804 (OC)
ISSNs: 2634-8772 (online), 2634-8764 (print)

Contents

1 Introduction   1

2 Male Femininity, Citizenship, and Democracy in the Linguistic Landscape of a "Pride" Protest in Bangkok   8

3 Spatializing the Intersections of Sexuality and Class in the Metro Manila Pride March   23

4 Challenging Heteronormativity and Reifying *Tai*-ness: The Linguistic Landscape of Taiwan LGBT+ Pride   35

5 "Asia's World City" as Homotopia? Surveying Tensions in the Linguistic Landscape of the Hong Kong Gay Games   62

6 Conclusion   74

7 Navigating Asian Pride from Sexual Citizenship and Governmentality Perspectives: Commentary by Mie Hiramoto   76

References   82

1 Introduction

Pride is a phenomenon that has reached well beyond its historical and political roots in post-Stonewall USA to become a truly global celebration of the LGBTQIA+ (Lesbian, Gay, Bisexual, Transgender, Queer/Questioning, Intersex, and Asexual etc.) movement. With Pride events and Pride-like movements now taking place in diverse areas of the world, we see various expressions of LGBTQIA+ solidarity that, while ostensibly tethered to Pride's historical and symbolic roots, have also taken on both regional and localized forms in accordance with the particular experiences and circumstances of each community. Given the variety of forms that Pride takes (e.g., political demonstrations, parades), Markwell and Waitt (2009) see an ideology of Pride informing and shaping most LGBTQIA+ festivals, explaining that these events are undergirded by a creative politics that opens "possibilities of novelty, new narratives and alternative futures" (p. 163). Pride events may therefore be thought of as polysemic rather than monolithic or inherently homogenous (Ammaturo, 2016). Simply put, and despite surface observations of commonality (e.g., the use of rainbow flags and universalizing slogans such as "Love is Love"), it is evident that Pride is neither a "one size fits all" phenomenon, nor, and more critically speaking with respect to this Element, simply a neocolonial imposition of Western value systems on "others" with different cultures and interests.

It is therefore with this understanding in mind that we assemble as sociolinguistic/discourse scholars who have research interests in how Pride is manifested and practiced in Asian contexts to provide a contemporary account and analysis of recent Pride(like) events in this region of the globe. To this end we traverse interrelated yet also distinct manifestations of Pride across, respectively, Thailand (Pavadee), the Philippines (Christian), Taiwan (Li-Chi), and Hong Kong (Ben) by bringing together aspects of individual projects we have recently conducted as situated researchers and residents in these locales. In doing so, our research on Pride draws on Gopinath's (2007, p. 343) notion of "an alternative mapping of sexual geographies that links disparate transnational regions"; an approach which attempts to move beyond what often appears to be a singular focus on either the local, or national, or the global (Chiang and Wong, 2016). Our collective aim under such an approach is therefore to unpack how ideologies of Pride may be appropriated, negotiated, and often reworked by people on the ground across these locales in their pursuit of alternative queer futures (i.e., futures that are not foretold under dominant Western discourses of LGBTQIA+ Pride but that are bound to particular sociohistorical flows in the building of more equitable, resilient, and sustainable communities).

Bringing together our research in this way means that we are able to establish a dialogue that encompasses points of theoretical and methodological synergy. This is a synergy that, in turn, leads, we hope, to a richer understanding of Pride in Asia and its significance as an indicator of LGBTQIA+ sociolinguistic action and stasis/change in the region. As such, we all work to various degrees in alignment with the approaches of linguistic (or semiotic) landscape (LL) research. Specifically, with our focus on Pride events, we are concerned with how language and other semiotic forms related to gender and sexuality, and their intersections with other social categories, are impacted by, interact with, and (re)shape the LL of public spaces (Borba and Hiramoto, 2024) with relation to the events we investigate. Most importantly, and as stated above, our work is incumbent upon a prioritization of the local vis-à-vis the transregional, as we seek to highlight sociolinguistic actions that are not always visible in a research field that is often dominated by Western-centric accounts and perspectives.

Accordingly, our LL research is presented here in dialogue with theoretical and methodological formations initiated through the interdisciplinary approaches of what may be loosely termed as queer Asian studies or "Asia as method" (Chen, 2010). As above, these approaches foreground local queer perspectives with the aim of provincializing hegemonic Western-derived theories of gender, sexuality, and social action, as well as addressing global imbalances in knowledge production and representation. Emphasizing transregional commitments and possibilities (Chiang and Wong, 2016), research in queer Asian studies recognizes not only extant commonalities across Asian regions but also the heterogeneities that incorporate diverse scales of queer sexualities related to flows of people, ideas, and actions toward a conceptual understanding of "Asias" in the plural (Ho and Blackwood, 2022) rather than a monolithic "Other" in counterpoint to the West. As a consequence of the drive to provincialize knowledge production from the West, scholars working within the approaches of queer Asian studies have sought to displace theory from high academia by building on understandings from those taking action on the ground (Luther and Loh, 2019).

In practice, working in alignment with such a position means that although we may draw upon concepts that have developed from post-structuralist Western (queer) theorizing, namely identity, intertextuality, intersectionality, sexual citizenship, and homonationalism, we seek to understand how these constructs may be understood and/or (re)imagined through Pride events via a local or transregional lens. A case in point is Puar's (2007) theory of homonationalism which was originally posited in response to the cynical co-option of Pride discourse by the US state to draw a distinction between the progressive and inclusive policies supposedly practiced by the West and the regressive, misogynistic, and homophobic policies of the enemy, in this case some Islamic states. In most of the Asian Pride events we cover here, we can certainly discern actions that might be labeled as homonationalist, in that the organizers seek to maximize the mutually beneficial relationship between the state and the LGBTQIA+ community. Yet, unlike Puar's concept of homonationalism, in these cases homonationalism is more a strategy from below, mobilized by people who often have to work in spaces of civic restriction, illiberalism, and authoritarianism (see also Lazar, 2017; Kong, 2023).

It is therefore by following this grounded approach, with all of us using participatory methods in our studies, that we aim to establish a transregional overview of Pride in Asia via our research narratives from a selection of Pride(like) events. Ultimately, this involves highlighting aspects of these Asian Pride movements where we see significant discursive and material overlaps in strategy, staging, and direction, and also particularities and peculiarities that demonstrate the significance of localness and the use of specific linguistic/semiotic resources to spread the message of LGBTQIA+ solidarity, equality, and legitimacy in the region.

In this introductory section then, we first provide the necessary background to Pride movements, along with a brief overview of LL research that has explored the significance of Pride events as gatherings of people who collectively aim to "queer" public spaces (Ammaturo, 2016). This section of the Element ends with an outline of the research contained herein. It is therefore our hope that by bringing together this research, we can establish more concretely and in greater detail the significance of linguistic/semiotic practices observed in Pride events in Asia that rework and often depart from globalizing LGBTQIA+ discursive flows. In this way, we expect our Element to provide readers with more expansive and inclusive conceptions of what Pride may mean to communities and in places outside of dominant Euro-American spheres of understanding and interpretation.

1.1 Researching and Understanding Pride Movements: Linguistic Landscape Approaches

Pride events stand as an enduring expression of the transnational LGBTQIA+ movement, providing opportunities for LGBTQIA+ people to gain visibility and legitimacy in their respective locales. Decades after the first Pride march in 1970, held in Christopher Street, New York, Pride and Pride-like movements have spread to urban and rural areas internationally, contributing to Pride's status as a symbol of the global struggle for LGBTQIA+ recognition (Markwell and Waitt, 2009; Ong, Lewis, and Vorobjovas-Pinta, 2021; Pak and Hiramoto,

2021; Rowlett and Go, 2024). According to Outright International (2021), ninety-two countries celebrated Pride in 2016. This number grew in 2022 with 105 countries holding Pride in their respective locales (Outright International, 2022). The growing number, in part, represents the continued role of Pride marches as a predominant platform for reaching out, creating visibility, and political claim-staking for different LGBTQIA+ communities. By marching in Pride parades, LGBTQIA+ people and their allies can claim public space in heteronormative dominant societies and build a collective bond with other members of the community (Engel, 2001).

While Pride marches within liberal and democratic domains of the Global North have largely taken on a celebratory tone, it is crucial to note that outside of these conducive environments, Pride assumes distinctive contours to manage social, political, and cultural norms and mores according to where such events take place. Adaptations of Pride in Asia, for example, which has sixteen member organizations affiliated with the international organization Interpride (2020), present a variety of opportunities for rethinking what Pride is and looks like in the countries of this region. In Singapore, for example, the annual Pink Dot event is held in a context where nearly all forms of public protest are outlawed. This means that the organizers have had to carefully strategize their rendering of Pride to align with governmental priorities regarding the traditional values that constitute good citizenship in Singapore. In practice, this involves the use of a nonconfrontational display of entertaining public engagement in place of Western-style protest marches (Phillips, 2013; Lazar, 2017; Rowlett and Go, 2024). Likewise, Pride in Phnom Penh highlights the carnivalesque in its Tuk Tuk Race, reflecting commercial and touristic forces that figure strongly in Cambodia's state sanctioned national imaginary (Rowlett and Go, 2024). Meanwhile, Shanghai Pride consisted of different activities, such as art and film exhibitions and themed talks rather than a public gathering, before being shut down in a climate of increasing censorship in Mainland China in 2020 (Jiang, 2020).

It is in this sense therefore, that one understanding of Pride in Asia might be reached via a transregional approach that is sensitive to discursive constructions of what Chua (2012) has theorized as "pragmatic resistance" (see also Rowlett and Go, 2024). Such acts of pragmatic resistance might therefore be read into how the organizers of Pride events in illiberal contexts, such as those above, are compelled to repurpose both ideologies of Pride and nationalist-oriented ideologies of good citizenship, resulting in discursive entanglements that tread a fine line between stating their cause and complying with societal and/or governmental expectations of what is or isn't permissible with respect to challenging the status quo. At the same time, however, and given the diverse sociocultural contexts we cover in this Element, we need to be wary of oversimplification in subscribing to dominant themes of commonality, recognizing that Pride, in the cases represented here, often intersects with broader, yet locally derived social movements and concerns.

In terms of researching Pride, it is understandable that these public-facing LGBTQIA+ events have provided rich sites for investigation in the field of language, gender, and sexuality, particularly from an LL perspective. Linguistic landscape is a field that draws from sociolinguistics and language policy to study how languages are visually displayed and hierarchized in multilingual societies. As Shohamy and Ben-Rafael (2015, p. 1) define it, LL is research focused on "the presence, representation, meanings and interpretation of languages displayed in public spaces." While this concern with the visibility of language in a given territory is the foundation of LL, such scholarship has also taken on a multimodal and multisemiotic orientation, reflecting a more holistic understanding of the relationship between language and other semiotic modes that constitute public space (Lazar, 2021). In this respect, LL analysis has extended to a consideration of, for example, the visual and corporeal, and the interplay between offline and online spaces (Maly and Blommaert, 2019). Especially pertinent to the examination of Pride events is an analytical focus in LL studies on how "spaces are themselves performed semiotically i.e. spaces accrue particular social meanings through the process of semiosis" (Lazar, 2021, p. 488). That is, in what ways does the use of meaning-making resources (signs, bodies, actions) create spaces for visibility and representations of LGBTQIA+ people?

In recent years there have been a number of gender/sexuality-related LL studies that investigate how semiotic processes facilitate the spatialization of sexuality. A few important examples include research on the use of English signage in the LL of Tokyo's gay district (Baudinette, 2013), and in the adult entertainment areas of Bangkok (Santos and Saisuwan, 2023), as well as on homonormative signage used in middle-class residential areas of the US (Motschenbacher, 2020b). On Pride events specifically, Milani (2015) used an LL approach to analyze the Johannesburg Pride Festival, arguing that Joburg Pride's claims to urban space are based on "an alignment with state-sanctioned, rights-based discourses of lesbian and gay identities," while counteractions in these urban spaces by the One in Nine Campaign (a queer activist group) can be seen as "spatial disruptions that problematise an overly optimistic reliance on sexual identities as catalysts for political action" (p. 436). In Singapore, Pak (2023) focuses on the offline/online nexus to investigate the circulability of Pink Dot counter discourse, through messages posted to a publicly accessible virtual map of the city. Meanwhile, Rowlett and Go's (2024) LL study of Phnom Penh

Pride illustrates the ways in which queer visibility and issues in an illiberal context are strategically made in conjunction with other discourses. These are commercial discourses of consumption and tourism, and international LGBTQIA+ discourse, that are brought together with the Cambodian government's discourse of national development and public health. At the same time, however, this strategy results, the authors suggest, in the privileging of certain LGBTQIA+ identities (e.g., gay and lesbian expatriates and tourists) over others (e.g., the urban poor).

In sum, all these studies illustrate the value of LL as a methodological/ analytical approach in elucidating and interrogating the role of sexuality in the discursive configuration of spatial contexts. Furthermore, these studies highlight how the visibility of sexuality within these spaces is intricately enmeshed in wider sociopolitical and cultural contexts and regimes of power. For example, one consequence of these entanglements is that the empowerment frequently associated with visibility can unintentionally perpetuate and establish hierarchies within communities marginalized due to their sexual orientation (Milani and Levon, 2016).

By building on many of these foundational insights, the research presented in this Element therefore aims to provide a transregional account, from an LL perspective, of more recent Pride events in Asian contexts. Methodologically speaking, our LL data encompasses, for the most part, the capture of audiovisual and textual data (signs, interactions, speeches, media reports) from each Pride event, which are analyzed qualitatively according to the semiotic processes (e.g., indexicality, stancetaking) that inform the linguistic/visual/discursive choices on display across both physical and online spaces. Additionally, our research operationalizes observational methods through on-site/online participation in the events (Pavadee, Christian, and Li-Chi) along with our perspectives as LGBTQIA+ community members with vested interests in the promotion and organization of local/international events (Ben). Our participatory orientations to the research are, in this way, aimed at harnessing the experiential qualities that go into the creation and formation of the LLs, where reflexive practices of "looking alongside" rather than "looking at" participants in the LL (Seals, 2017) have allowed us to gain insights from multiple perspectives. In turn, these methodological practices have enabled us, in accordance with approaches from queer Asian studies, to provide a grounded analysis in our respective sections – one that is aware of historical and social developments in each context, alongside sensitivities with relation to locally specific ways of knowing and doing.

1.2 Preview of Sections

We begin with Pavadee Saisuwan's study in the Thai context which investigates the LL of the first LGBTQIA+-led pro-democracy protest that took place in Bangkok in 2020. The analysis involves examining signage, speeches, and activities during the protest through the lens of the three semiotic processes of iconization, fractal recursivity, and erasure (Irvine and Gal, 2000). The findings demonstrate the prominence of male femininity or *kathoey*ness in various linguistic resources, including lexical choice and intertextuality. While other LGBTQIA+ identities received less acknowledgment, there was a differentiation between LGBTQIA+ and non-LGBTQIA+ individuals, who united in an alliance for democracy against "dictatorship." The LL of the protest highlights how *kathoey*ness was used as an icon representing and embracing Thai LGBTQIA+ people of diverse identities. It created an inclusive space within the protest and allowed Thai LGBTQIA+ communities to assert their identities not only as LGBTQIA+ individuals but also as Thai citizens.

In the following section, Christian Go investigates the ways in which the 2023 Metro Manila Pride march (MM Pride) is constructed as a space for intersectional LGBTQIA+ activism. Using photographic data he collected during the event, the section examines the deployment of discursive and semiotic resources and the concomitant stances that MM Pride participants take up in their representational tools (e.g., banners, placards, clothing). The stances exhibit adaptation and negotiation of discourses concerning sexual identity politics as well as socioeconomic and political issues. The agglomeration of these discourses in the LL reflects MM Pride's evolution as a platform for intersectional advocacy and solidarity. This section therefore contributes to the understanding of how a Pride march in an Asian context offers an entry point into understanding how intersectional discourse motivates alternative imaginings of Pride and a collective push for visibility, inclusivity, and social change.

The next section details an LL analysis of Taiwan LGBT+ Pride from 2010 to 2020 by Li-Chi Chen. The analytical focus is on how heteronormativity is challenged and how Taiwanese localness (i.e., *tai*-ness) is reified in Pride slogans and fashion. The findings suggest that Taiwanese Pride marchers challenge heteronormativity through homonormative practices, the discursive construction of sexual desire, the struggle against traditional Confucianism, the redefinition of masculinity, and the marginalization of heterosexuality. On the other hand, they were found to reify *tai*-ness through the construction of dual identities, the application of local semiotics, the participation in issues of social justice, and the use of mockery as shared humor. These strategies were used by LGBTQIA+ Taiwanese to negotiate their local identities as multiethnic and humorous queer Taiwanese and their global identities as knowledgeable sexual moderns. The diachronic data also revealed the intersections between Pride and the social problems that Taiwan has faced over the past decade.

The final context of Pride covered in this Element departs somewhat from on-site LL research on Pride events to focus on the discursive construction of place vis-à-vis the Gay Games in Hong Kong. In this section, Ben Rowlett draws on the notion of "homotopia," as used in sociolinguistic studies of sexuality and sexual citizenship in relation to space and place, to interpret a survey and critical discourse analysis of the (online) LL of the Gay Games, an international LGBTQIA+ mass-scale sporting and cultural event, which was held in Asia for the first time in November 2023. The analysis focuses on the tensions that emerge within this LL, particularly in relation to entanglements of socio- and geopolitical discourses of Pride, nationalism, security, and (sexual) citizenship.

After a short conclusion that brings together all sections, our Element wraps up with a commentary by Mie Hiramoto. In her commentary, Mie adds her own perspective to the findings of this research and the ongoing significance of sociolinguistic studies of LGBTQIA+ public-facing events in Asia and beyond.

2 Male Femininity, Citizenship, and Democracy in the Linguistic Landscape of a "Pride" Protest in Bangkok

In this first section, I (Pavadee) focus on *Mob mai mungming tae tungting kha khun ratthaban* "Not a cutesy mob but a flamboyant one, sir, Mr. Government," which was the first LGBTQIA+-led pro-democracy protest that took place in Bangkok in 2020. Unlike previous political protests, this movement had a Pride-like atmosphere, incorporating elements from queer culture and pop culture, making it unique to the pro-democracy movement in Thailand. By considering the signage and activities during the protests as part of semiotic assemblages (Pennycook, 2017), my objective is to explore how Thai LGBTQIA+ communities utilized linguistic resources within the LL of the protest to express their citizenship (Isin, 2017) in the localized form of pro-democracy "Pride" protests. Using the analytical framework of three semiotic processes: iconization, fractal recursivity, and erasure (Irvine and Gal, 2000), my analysis reveals the underlying ideologies present in the protest and the significance of male femininity or *kathoey*ness in contributing to the inclusivity advocated by the protest.

Thai society has displayed considerable engagement in promoting gender equality and related issues. In Thai LGBTQIA+ movements, as in other societies worldwide, the principles of equality and inclusivity have played a central role, notably showcased through Pride events. The focus on LGBTQIA+ rights in Thailand predominantly revolves around the interests of LGBTQIA+

communities and activists. Despite the growing awareness within society, this concern remains somewhat detached from mainstream Thai politics. However, in 2020, Thai LGBTQIA+ communities made a significant stride in Thai national politics. They spearheaded Pride-like protests that intersected with other demonstrations addressing political and royal reform, equality, and human rights, thus elevating their visibility and impact.

With a focus on the pro-democracy protest, I address the concept of citizenship with relation to the LL. In line with previous research (e.g., Milani, 2015; Milani and Levon, 2016; Milani et al., 2018), I examine the intersection between the LL, sexuality, and citizenship. The protest is considered an act of performative citizenship (Isin, 2017), as the protesters, by participating in the movement, assert their rights as citizens of the country. Furthermore, as Richardson (1998, p. 88) argues, "claims to citizenship status, at least in the West, are closely associated with the institutionalisation of heterosexual, as well as male, privilege." The movement led by LGBTQIA+ communities in Bangkok also engages with the concept of sexual citizenship, which is defined in terms of sexual rights (Richardson, 2000).

Adopting the concept of sexual citizenship within the protest demonstrates how Thai LGBTQIA+ communities align with their counterparts worldwide through Pride-like movements. Altman (1997) argues that sexual citizenship relies on rights shared across national and cultural boundaries and presumes universally recognized forms of homosexual or transgender identities, leading to the concept of global sexual citizenship, which assumes homogenization. This is reflected in the Pride movement, which has become a global phenomenon connecting people with diverse gender and sexual identities from various contexts. The movement enables these individuals to move in the same direction as an imagined community, despite their differences. Jackson (2004) claims that there was no homosexual rights movement in Thailand, which undermines the idea of global sexual citizenship. The protest under study here demonstrates the progress in Thai society over the past twenty years, as LGBTQIA+ people have united and expressed a standpoint that is not only national but also aligned with the global Pride movement and the concept of global sexual citizenship.

Despite aligning with the global movement, the term *gay*, which is adopted from the West and associated with modernization and participation in the international sphere (Jackson, 2004), is not prevalent in the protest. The localness of the protest under study lies in the use of a local gender category and the local performance of male femininity as important resources As will be shown later in this section, the identity of *kathoey* (male-to-female transgenders in Thailand) is a significant part of the protest. Male femininity, or effeminacy, is considered central to the gender identity performance of Thai *kathoey* and gay men. According to Duangwises and Jackson (2021), femininity is not exclusive to women and male-to-female transgenders in Thai society but can be adopted by gay men depending on the social context. Effeminacy does not carry the same negative perception for gay men as it does in the West and is associated with "playful bitchiness" (Duangwises and Jackson, 2021, p. 10). This provides an opportunity for Thai LGBTQIA+ communities to use various resources associated with male femininity to make a powerful statement or an impactful assertion during the protest.

2.1 Pro-Democracy Protests in Thailand in 2020

The year 2020 was an important time in Thai politics. A series of protests led by different groups of people took place across the country. This pro-democracy movement was built up from people's dissatisfaction with the "undemocratic" election in 2019, which resulted in the pro-military government, originally the coup government of 2014. The series of protests began in earnest after the constitutional court's decision to dissolve the Future Forward Party, one of the main opposition parties, and ban its leaders from politics for ten years. In addition, the outbreak of COVID-19 exacerbated dissatisfaction with the government's ineffective management, leading to continuous protests. The anti-government protests not only expressed dissatisfaction with the government of the time, calling for its resignation, but also included demands for constitutional reform and monarchy reform.

University and high school students both played a leading role in the 2020 pro-democracy movement. The student activist group Bad Student started with demands based on the school context, such as school uniforms and hairstyles and the education system (see Kraijariyawet, 2021). Their movement also touched on values that have long been influential in Thai society, such as gratitude, patriarchy, and authoritarianism. The student-led protests later broadened to include issues beyond the school context, such as equality and freedom of expression. They are also part of the movement calling for reform of the monarchy. The protests, including those organized by Free Youth and the United Front of Thammasat and Demonstration (UFTD) in 2020, are believed to be the first time in Thai history that students have organized large-scale protests against the monarchy (Lertchoosakul, 2021).

The pro-democracy protests that took place in Thailand in 2020 took a different form from the pro-democracy protests of the past. The protests were organized as flash mobs, sometimes simultaneously in different places, both in Bangkok and other provinces, rather than as prolonged protests. They were also leaderless, which made the protests agile and effective without requiring long advanced planning (Sinpongsaporn, 2020). The success of these flash mobs and leaderless protests was made possible by the use of social media, which was an important communication tool in the protests. The use of social media allowed people to share their ideas and join the movement wherever they were, so participation in the protests was not limited to those who were physically present (see Akkaravisitpol, 2021; Intorn, 2021; Thanapornsangsuth and Anamwathana, 2022).

One of the most influential social media platforms in the Thai 2020 pro-democracy protests was Twitter, now known as X. Sinpeng (2021) sees the use of Twitter hashtags as hashtag activism, bringing together both activists and ordinary people in the movement. Sinpeng (2021) claims that the main purpose of using Twitter was to construct shared stories, including dissatisfaction with the government, issues related to democracy and youth rights, and to spread information related to the movement, rather than to organize and promote offline protest actions.

One of the student-led protests that garnered significant attention both in physical spaces and on social media was *Mob mai mungming tae tungting kha khun ratthaban* "Not a cutesy mob but a flamboyant one, sir, Mr. Government," which was a series of LGBTQIA+-led protests initiated by Free Gender TH, a group of Thai LGBTQIA+ activists. The protest under examination in this section is the first one that occurred on July 25, 2020. However, the series also includes two additional protests. The second one took place in November of the same year, also in Bangkok, while the third one was organized online in 2021 due to the spread of COVID-19.

This LGBTQIA+-led protest marks an important milestone in Thai political history as it is considered the first time that Thai LGBTQIA+ communities played a leading role in national politics. At the first protest, protest leaders issued a statement supporting the demands made earlier by Free Youth, which included a new constitution, the dissolution of parliament, and an end to the state's intimidation of its people. The protest also touched on other LGBTQIA+-related issues, including the legalization of same-sex marriage, sex workers, and abortion. The protesters demonstrated that the demand for gender equality and acceptance of sexual diversity could not be achieved in an undemocratic society, highlighting the need for the pro-democracy movement and the LGBTQIA+ movement to work together in tandem.

Another noticeable feature of the protest was the Pride-like atmosphere, which set it apart from other typical political protests which are usually more solemn in nature. The protest incorporated queer culture and Pride symbols such as rainbow flags to create an enjoyable experience and to demonstrate that roles in politics are not exclusively for men (see Chuipracha, 2020). Elements of

Thai pop culture often associated with the LGBTQIA+ community were used not only to create an entertaining experience but also to effectively communicate the issues and underscore the demands.

2.2 Citizenship and Linguistic Landscape

Political protest is seen as a form of performative citizenship. Performative citizenship (Isin, 2017) refers to the ways in which individuals and social groups claim their rights and demonstrate their right to claim their rights. It involves social or political struggles of both citizens and noncitizens. Certain groups of people are more dominant than others, while certain groups are not fully accepted as citizens. Since the boundaries between these different statuses are not fixed, struggles for rights involve exercising rights, claiming one's rights, and claiming for and against the rights of others.

Linguistic landscape studies have demonstrated the connection between space, citizenship, and sexuality. Milani (2015) introduces the concept of "sexual cityzenship" to emphasize the spatial aspect of sexuality. Based on his research conducted during Joburg Pride 2012, he illustrates how perspectives on sexual politics are tied to the national identity of being South African. The Pride event space allows for the expression of both pride and shame, indicating "an emotionally ambivalent act of citizenship" (Milani, 2015, p. 447). Similarly, Milani et al. (2018) reveal that sexuality is utilized to contribute to national identity, both by supporting the state's homonationalism and by condemning pinkwashing in Israel. Moreover, graffiti in Athens and Belgrade illustrates the association of homophobic ideas with nationalism and religion (Canakis and Kersten-Pejanić, 2016). These studies highlight diverse ways in which citizenship and sexuality intersect and are interconnected.

The Thai LGBTQIA+-led protest analyzed in this section exemplifies an act of citizenship undertaken by Thai LGBTQIA+ communities. The protesters not only advocated for LGBTQIA+-related issues but also demonstrated solidarity with other social groups by supporting their demands pertaining to national political matters. This affirms the position of LGBTQIA+ communities as Thai citizens and highlights the interconnection between LGBTQIA+ rights and democracy, thereby showcasing the intersectionality of gender, sexuality, and national identity, a recurrent theme which is also analyzed in the sections on Metro Manila and Taiwan Pride events (Section 3 and Section 4).

My research examines the use of diverse linguistic resources with the objective of revealing the underlying ideologies within the act of citizenship carried out during the protest. Since the protest was led by Thai LGBTQIA+

communities, I address the topics of gender and sexuality in LL studies, which have predominantly centered around multilingual signage in Thai academia. Furthermore, it aligns with prior LL studies that explore the connection between citizenship and national political movements within the broader scope of LL analysis.

2.3 Data Collection and Analytical Framework

The data I analyzed in this section were collected from *Mob mai mungming tae tungting kha khun ratthaban* "Not a cutesy mob but a flamboyant one, sir, Mr. Government," a protest held at the Democracy Monument in Bangkok on July 25, 2020. In terms of the timeline, the protest commenced with a statement by Free Gender TH, the protest organizer, which supported the demands previously made by Free Youth and addressed LGBTQIA+-related issues such as the legalization of same-sex marriage. Following the statement, various activists delivered speeches covering diverse topics, including the legalization of sex work, rights of trans women and conscription, and the relationship between LGBTQIA+ rights and democracy. The final segment of the protest involved a role-play inspired by a popular Thai film, as well as recreational dancing. These activities were conducted as group activities with the active participation of the protesters.

In this research I adopt a broad interpretation of LL data, including not only signage but also speeches and activities that were integral to the protest. An approximately two-hour recording of the protest was made available on the YouTube channel of Prachatai, a Thai online newspaper. The recording captures the speeches and statements made at the beginning of the protest and the activities in which the protesters participated at the end of the protest. Images of the protest's signage were taken from online news articles and the Twitter hashtag associated with the protest, which is the same as the name of the protest. The hashtag was joined by both official online news agency accounts and personal accounts. Images include those of physical signage used in the protest and online media posted on Twitter to promote the protest.

To uncover the underlying ideologies in the protest, I employ the three semiotic processes outlined by Irvine and Gal (2000). Iconization is the process by which a particular feature becomes associated with a specific social group. This association transforms the feature into an icon representing the social group, and it is perceived as inherent and essential. Fractal recursivity involves the repetition of binary oppositions across different levels of categorization. Erasure is a process whereby certain individuals or entities are deliberately disregarded or rendered invisible to enhance the intelligibility of the ideological perception. This framework is used to analyze how different groups of people were depicted in relation to one another within the LL of the protest, shedding light on the relationship between Thai LGBTQIA+ communities, citizenship, and their advocacy for democracy.

2.4 Analysis

In this analysis, I demonstrate the use of various linguistic resources in different segments of the protest to illustrate the prominence of male femininity or *kathoey*ness. While the protest involved a diverse range of participants aligning with LGBTQIA+ communities, linguistic elements associated with the *kathoey* identity were highly notable and served as significant tools during the protest.

One of the most intriguing aspects that sets this protest apart from others is its title, *Mob mai mungming tae tungting kha khun ratthaban*, usually translated in the news as "Not a cutesy mob but a flamboyant one, sir, Mr. Government." Prior to this protest, there were other pro-democracy demonstrations led and attended by school students, which a government supporter referred to as *mungming* "cute, adorable," implying a sense of childishness and lack of seriousness. In solidarity with those previous pro-democracy protests, this LGBTQIA+-led protest made it explicit in the title that they were not *mungming*. The protest's identity was clarified through the use of the term *tungting* "effeminate," which conveys flamboyance and is associated with male effeminacy and *kathoey*ness. Derived from *kratung krating*, the term is most commonly used to refer to effeminate men or *kathoey* (Jackson, 2004). Additionally, the title incorporates the feminine polite final particle *kha*, emphasizing the feminine expression of the protests, and addresses the government with the polite term *khun*, which is gender-neutral in Thai. These polite elements are represented as "sir" and "Mr." in the English translation. The protest title characterizes the individuals initiating the protests and brings visibility to the *kathoey* identity.

The *kathoey* identity was explicitly referenced in various parts of the protest. Figure 1 displays one of the messages written on a cloth that provided a space for protesters to express their thoughts during the protest. The message states, *Mob si sotsai kathoey thai cha pen yai nai phaendin* "Vibrant and shining, Thai *kathoey* will prevail across the land." Figure 2 presents one of the promotional materials that was shared on Twitter by Raptor, one of the protest organizers. The text reads, *I tu (tukkata) tolae! Tae kathoey chat mop ching mai tolae* "Tu (the doll), you liar! But *kathoey* will really lead a protest, not liars here." This was inspired by the film series *Hor taew tak* "Haunting me," which was an important source of intertextuality in the protest.

Figure 1 "Vibrant and shining, Thai *kathoey* will prevail across the land" (Rinna pa Pepsi thung, 2020).

Figure 2 "Tu (the doll), you liar! But *kathoey* will really lead a protest, not liars here" (Raptor eng cha, 2020).

Hor taew tak is a popular Thai comedy film series that debuted on the screen in 2007. It prominently features *kathoey* characters and has become strongly associated with the *kathoey* community. Because of this association, the protesters drew inspiration from components in the film and incorporated them into the protest in a parodic manner. The protest organizers distributed scripts from two significant scenes in the film to the protesters, encouraging them to participate in the parodic activity.

One of the scenes used by the protesters was "the doll," where two characters, Pancake and Taew, are engaged in a conversation. In the original scene, Pancake uses profanity directed at Taew, claiming that she was referring to her doll named Taew, not the person Taew. Excerpt 1 represents the modified script used in the protest. The name of the doll was changed from Taew to Tu, which was the nickname of the country's prime minister at that time. During the protest, the organizers showcased a plastic model named Tu. Whenever they used profanity directed at Tu, they asserted that they were referring to the model or "the doll" and not the prime minister. The image in the background of the promotional material in Figure 2 was also taken from the scene.

Excerpt 1

MC:	I tu
	"Tu"
Everyone:	I tolae
	"You liar"
Everyone:	I tu, i tolae x 5 khrang
	"Tu, you liar x 5 times"
MC:	Ha! Mueng da nayok roe
	"What? You mean the PM?"
Everyone:	Da tukkata!
	"I mean the doll!"
MC:	O laeo pai
	"Oh, okay"

Excerpt 1 serves as an example of parodied recontextualization (Hodges, 2015). The protesters drew inspiration from a conversation in the film and integrated it into the protest activity. The original version, which was not initially connected to politics, was adapted to fulfil political objectives in the protest. The parodied version effectively displayed the protesters' lack of respect toward the prime minister at that time, who became the center of mockery within this recontextualized conversation.

Another example of intertextuality is the poem shown in Excerpt 2, another instance of *kathoey*-associated resources used in the protest. Originally, the poem served as part of a question in Miss ACDC, a pageant for male-to-female transgender individuals that parodies female beauty pageants. The question asked, "What are the three miracles that would make this poem come true?" The poem gained popularity and was repurposed for political contexts, including in this LGBTQIA+-led protest. Toward the end of the protest, one of the organizers recited this poem, stating that the three miracles to be sought include a new constitution, the dissolution of parliament, and an end to the state's intimidation of its people, which were the three demands of the protesters. This demonstrates how the poem was recontextualized and reinterpreted in the context of the political protest. This instance highlights yet another use of resources associated with *kathoey*ness and further underscores the prominence of *kathoey* in the protest.

> **Excerpt 2**
> *Nai thisut rao ko mi thi yat yuen*
> "Here is our place to stand"
>
> *Salat thing lok khomkhuen thi lalang*
> "Leaving behind the old suffering world"
>
> *Ma ruam yattra thap rak seri mi phalang*
> "Come join the army of love"
>
> *Chut fai wang sang lok mai hai sophi*
> "Let's light up the world"

Feminine linguistic features were evident in the speech delivered during the protest. Excerpt 3 was taken from Raptor's speech at the start of the protest, which demonstrates their use of feminine linguistic features (highlighted in bold). The feminine polite final particle *kha* was employed, mirroring the use in the protest's title. Raptor also used the feminine pronoun *dichan*, which serves as a significant marker of femininity among *kathoey* speakers (Saisuwan, 2016).

> **Excerpt 3**
> *To hai sing thi **dichan** phut ma thangmot ni man cha na sao lae ko na sin wang khanat nai na **kha** tae wanni thi **dichan** ma yuen yu trongni wanni **dichan** yak cha yuenyan **kha** phrowa **dichan** yang chuea lae sattha yu samoe wa prathet khong rao cha tong di khuen cha tong mi phap na **kha** khong futbat thi **dichan** sai son sung hok nio lae doen nai sadut dai **kha***

"No matter how sad or hopeless the things **I**'ve mentioned are, but today, **I** stand here, today **I** want to make a confirmation, because **I** still believe and always have believed that our country will be better. There will be footpaths that will allow **me** to walk in shoes with 6-inch heels without stumbling."

In addition to these linguistic elements, Raptor drew a connection between male femininity and national politics by expressing their belief in the potential for Thailand to improve. They envisioned a future where they can confidently walk in high-heeled shoes without stumbling on footpaths, which are notorious for their poor quality and represent the deficiencies in Thai politics, as asserted by the pro-democracy movement. Given that *kathoey*ness is ideologically linked to humor in Thai society, its use creates a stark contrast between the playful LGBTQIA+ characteristics and the conventional seriousness associated with the political domain. The use of *kathoey*-associated resources enables the protesters to convey their demands in a playful and sarcastic manner, ultimately amplifying their impact.

The diverse elements employed in the protest demonstrate the crucial role of male femininity within this LGBTQIA+-led movement. The *kathoey* identity, once heavily stigmatized and marginalized in Thai society, has become an emblem for Thai LGBTQIA+ communities. The use of resources associated with *kathoey*ness was not intended to exclude other genders or sexualities, despite initial perceptions. Rather, the *kathoey* identity serves as a powerful symbol representing LGBTQIA+ individuals of various identities. Positioned at the opposite end of the "*Kathoey* – Gay – Man" model (Jackson, 1997), *kathoey*ness emerges as the most prominent nonnormative identity among Thai LGBTQIA+ communities, standing in stark contrast to men who seemingly dominate mainstream Thai national politics. Such status facilitates the process of iconizing *kathoey*ness in the LL of the protest. The incorporation of *kathoey*ness in the protest holds significant meaning, effectively addressing both LGBTQIA+ issues and national politics, serving the protest's objectives adeptly.

The iconization of *kathoey*ness inevitably contributes to the erasure of other LGBTQIA+ identities. The *kathoey* identity was highly visible in the protest, while other LGBTQIA+ identities were much less visible. This raised questions among the protesters. As shown in Excerpt 4, an event MC asked Raptor if it was true that only *kathoey* were participating in the protest. In their response, Raptor mentioned that the protest welcomed people of all genders, sexualities, and ages. This shows that the protest organizers were aware of the prominence of the *kathoey* identity in the protest and suggests that this did not imply exclusivity in terms of the identities of the protesters. Instances of the feminine polite final particle mentioned above have also been highlighted in bold.

Excerpt 4

MC: Khun phi **kha** nai wanni na **kha** lai khon ko du cha songsai wa mob khong rao mi tae kathoei ching mai **kha** khun phi **kha**

"Sister, today many people seem to wonder if our protest is only joined by *kathoey*. Is it true, sister?"

Raptor: Mai ching loei **kha** mob khong rao na **kha** mi tonrap thuk phet thuk wai loei na **kha** chahendaiwa rao mi baep wa phinong na **kha** thi wa ma chak oe ma chak lai klum attalak thang phet na **kha** ruam thueng lai klum chuang ayu duai

"Not true at all. Our protest welcomes every gender/sexuality of any age. You can see that we have friends from various groups of gender/sexual identity including various age groups."

As the protest was part of the broader pro-democracy movement, it involved the process of fractal recursivity, indicating the repetition of binary opposition across different levels. This includes the opposition between democracy and dictatorship, as well as the distinction between LGBTQIA+ individuals and non-LGBTQIA+ identities among those who identify with democracy.

The underlying opposition between democracy and dictatorship was evident. LGBTQIA+ communities were portrayed as standing in opposition to the "dictatorship," referring to the ruling government led by the prime minister, who had originally come to power through a coup in 2014. The message on the sign in Figure 3, which reads *klum queer mai lia phadetkan* "We queer don't lick

Figure 3 "We queer don't lick dictatorship's boots" (Hawae, 2020).

Figure 4 "I love dicks, not dictators" (Chuipracha, 2020).

dictatorship's boots," clearly indicates that the queer community positioned itself on the opposing side to the "dictatorship." Similarly, the message "I love dicks, not dictators" on the T-shirt in Figure 4 shows the rejection of the "dictatorship." The message cleverly plays with the shared pronunciation of the word "dicks" and the first syllable of the word "dictators." Given that the T-shirt is held by an individual who is perceived as male, the message can be interpreted as representative of male homosexual individuals. Furthermore, the message presented in Figure 1 earlier also highlights this opposition, as the *kathoey* identity is juxtaposed against "Tu," which was intended to reference the prime minister at that time. These examples showcase the alignment of LGBTQIA+ communities with democracy.

Despite the prominence of *kathoey*ness and the potential overshadowing of other LGBTQIA+ identities, it is important to note that, as shown in Raptor's confirmation in Excerpt 4, those who participated in the protest in support of democracy were not exclusively *kathoey* or LGBTQIA+ individuals. Figure 5 demonstrates a differentiation between *kathoey* and men or a non-LGBTQIA+ identity. It depicts a sign attached to drums, with Thai scripts written in the Lu language. The Lu language is a form of language play or secret language utilized among Thai *kathoey* speakers. The message on the sign reads, *len pun lu phi lai chui la mu luai chui ka loei thui*, which is derived from the Thai phrase *pen phuchai ma chuai kathoey*, meaning "I am a man who comes to assist *kathoey*." It is possible that this message was conveyed by drummers, who

Figure 5 "I am a man who comes to assist *kathoey*" (Mono News, 2020).

identified as men. This highlights the usage of another linguistic tool associated with the *kathoey* identity. It emphasizes the prevalence of *kathoey*ness and showcases the involvement of a non-LGBTQIA+ identity playing a supporting role within the LGBTQIA+-led movement.

Apart from *kathoey*ness and a non-LGBTQIA+ identity, other LGBTQIA+ identities, including bisexuals, transgenders, queers, lesbians, and *tom* (Thai female-to-male transgender individuals), were also acknowledged in the protest. These identities were present on signs and mentioned by the protesters. This demonstrates the inclusivity of the protest, as emphasized by Raptor. In other words, although other LGBTQIA+ identities were much less visible, they were not completely erased in the LL of the protest.

Adopting the three semiotic processes of iconization, fractal recursivity, and erasure (Irvine and Gal, 2000), my analysis has revealed how various linguistic resources were used in this Thai LGBTQIA+-led protest, reflecting underlying ideas concerning LGBTQIA+ communities and democracy in Thai society. Diverse linguistic elements associated with male femininity or *kathoey*ness, including the use of the term "kathoey," were employed. *Kathoey*ness dominated the LL of the protest, serving as an icon for Thai LGBTQIA+ identities. The *kathoey* identity was presented in contrast to a non-LGBTQIA+ identity within the LL of the protest. Alongside other LGBTQIA+ identities, they demonstrated support for democracy and opposition to the "dictatorship" represented by the government in power. While the protest witnessed participation from people of various identities, the *kathoey* identity stood out as the most prominent, while other identities remained less visible. These other identities were occasionally mentioned during the protest but were largely erased from signage. In other words, this Thai LGBTQIA+-led protest illustrates the iconization of *kathoey*ness, the fractal recursivity between dictatorship and democracy, and between the *kathoey* identity and a non-LGBTQIA+ identity, as well as the erasure of other LGBTQIA+ identities.

2.5 Conclusion

In this section I investigated the LL of the first LGBTQIA+-led pro-democracy protest in Bangkok. Through the lens of the three semiotic processes (Irvine and Gal, 2000), my analysis reveals the prominence of male femininity or *kathoey*ness alongside other LGBTQIA+ and non-LGBTQIA+ identities. It is argued that *kathoey*ness serves as a powerful resource to unite various LGBTQIA+ identities and foster inclusivity within the protest. The unique expression and presentation, typical among *kathoey*, represent Thai LGBTQIA+ communities and show a stark contrast with the typically patriarchal domain of Thai politics. As a Thai LGBTQIA+ identity, *kathoey*ness plays a significant role, becoming a shared and important tool among LGBTQIA+ individuals participating in the movement.

The use of *kathoey*ness provides an opportunity for Thai LGBTQIA+ individuals to assert their citizenship performatively (Isin, 2017). The protesters embraced *kathoey*ness as a representation of their LGBTQIA+ identities and used it to convey their political standpoint as Thai LGBTQIA+ individuals. The movement plays a significant role in making Thai LGBTQIA+ people more visible in the realm of Thai national politics, which has previously been predominantly exclusive to heterosexual individuals, particularly heterosexual men. This demonstrates that LGBTQIA+-related issues are not marginal or disconnected from other national political matters but rather constitute meaningful contributions to the democratic aspirations of the Thai people.

In addition to asserting their citizenship through *kathoey*ness, this Pride-like pro-democracy protest also showcases how Thai LGBTQIA+ communities aligned with the global Pride movement in a broad sense while maintaining their distinct local identity to express their political stance. This particular approach holds significant meaning, in common with the other Pride events examined in this Element, as it demonstrates the intersectionality of gender, sexuality, and national identity, highlighting how Thai LGBTQIA+ communities were able to simultaneously engage on both national and international levels through the LL of the protest. It also emphasizes the significance of localness while simultaneously showing solidarity with the global LGBTQIA+ movement.

3 Spatializing the Intersections of Sexuality and Class in the Metro Manila Pride March

In this section, I (Christian) examine the semiotic construction of Metro Manila Pride (MM Pride), focusing on how its politics manifest in the event's LL. By analysing the signs displayed at MM Pride 2023, I expand on Pavadee's preceding section to show how participants spatialize sexuality and highlight intersecting issues with LGBTQIA+ concerns, thereby fostering a localized and sustained form of activism. I engage with Conway's (2023) provocation in his work on Migrant Pride in Hong Kong, which emphasizes the need to scrutinize how radical queer politics are often overshadowed by capitalist agendas that privilege certain LGBTQIA+ lifestyles. Building on this, I explore how the discourses present in MM Pride's LL reveal it as a site for intersectional activism, where sexual identity politics intersect with broader social struggles. I demonstrate how MM Pride reinforces a regime of truths by foregrounding issues of sexual identity alongside issues of class and national concerns (Foucault, 2001; Conway, 2023). This highlights the "international connectedness yet local uniqueness" of localized Pride events such as MM Pride, which facilitate, draw on, and reproduce understandings of identity and sociopolitical change (Plummer, 1992). The regime of truths within MM Pride intersects with discourses of sexuality and social justice and creates a platform that brings the shared experiences of injustice and precarity among diverse minority groups to the forefront. This multiplicity defines local Pride politics and fosters solidarity through collective struggle while keeping Pride anchored in sexual identity.

MM Pride is an annual LGBTQIA+ event held in various cities in the metropolitan area. Like other Pride and Pride-like events discussed in this Element, it serves as a vehicle to raise the community's visibility, celebrate its achievements, and engage in sociopolitical action. A core component of MM Pride has been its sustained efforts to work with city governments in creating anti-discrimination ordinances as well as to advocate for the passage of a comprehensive SOGIESC (Sexual Orientation, Gender Identity, Gender Expression, or Sex Characteristics) bill at the national level. To understand MM Pride's underlying politics, it is crucial to note its roots in both local protest and community celebration. The origins of the event trace back to 1996 when it was organized by the Reach Out AIDS Foundation (Paradela, 2019). This version of Pride focused on showcasing the LGBTQIA+ community's diversity and fostering a sense of unity through a festival-like atmosphere, where in-group members were socialized into adopting community advocacies. However, a precursor to this event was Stonewall Manila in 1994, organized by the progressive group ProGay Philippines and the Metropolitan Manila Church (Evangelista, 2017). Unlike the celebratory tone of MM Pride, Stonewall Manila took the form of a public demonstration, marking the first deliberate adoption of Western (i.e., American) Pride discourse in the Philippines. In their manifesto, Stonewall Manila's organizers connected the unique struggles faced by working-class Filipino gays and lesbians – such as the implementation of additional taxes on goods and services and unregulated oil prices – with the historic 1969 Stonewall Riots in New York City, thus positioning their protest alongside a broader LGBTQIA+ movement (Evangelista, 2017). This dual character of MM Pride is present in its 2023 iteration where calls to combat social, economic, and political injustices are made alongside recognition of members of the LGBTQIA+ community. To explore these aspects of MM Pride, this section seeks to answer the following questions: (1) What kinds of discourses are represented in the signage at MM Pride? (2) How do stances on these discourses facilitate an emergent form of activism at MM Pride? To answer these questions, I draw on the notion of stance/stancetaking to analyze the semiotic strategies employed in signs that challenge or reproduce dominant discourses.

3.1 Stance

Du Bois (2007, p. 163) defines stance as "a public act by a social actor, achieved dialogically through overt communicative means ... through which social actors simultaneously evaluate objects, position subjects (themselves and others), and align with other subjects, with respect to any salient dimension of the sociocultural field." Simply put, stance is a multimodal construal that involves the combination of verbal and nonverbal resources (Pelclová, 2023). Du Bois' (2007, p. 139) model of stance identifies three dimensions: evaluation (to confer judgment upon the object of the stance), position (to orient oneself vis-à-vis the object being evaluated), and alignment (to fine-tune the alignment among those taking a stance). These dimensions underscore the role of stance in the management of social interactions, the production and reproduction of social meanings within a given society, and the construction and representation of identity (Bucholtz and Hall, 2010; Kiesling, 2022). Stance has been productively employed in understanding sexual identification. For instance, in Marino's (2023) research on Two-Spirit identity construction on TikTok, the author highlights how users effectively employ both linguistic and nonlinguistic cues to adopt specific stances that disavow gender-binary norms, heteronormative ideals within Western LGBTQIA+ discourse, and the dominant practice of labeling, while asserting their Two-Spirit identity. Meanwhile, Su's (2023) research on the marriage equality discussions in Taiwan highlights how bloggers strategically adopt the identity of a mother to assert a stance, effectively leveraging this position to promote certain ideologies (such as emphasizing the role of mothers in shaping their children's futures as opposed to relying solely on lawmakers) in favor of marriage equality. Such studies exemplify the growing focus within sociocultural linguistics on the evaluative, affective, and interpersonal aspects of stancetaking through the lens of sexuality. This section adopts a stance as a lens to analyze how signs in the LL represent stances that reproduce and negotiate discourses to articulate an alternative mode of LGBTQIA+ activism in intersectional terms.

This section analyzes the stances expressed through signs within MM Pride's LL to illuminate how local and localized discourses on sexuality, class, etc. are materialized in and through microlevel practices. By examining these sign-based stances, I demonstrate how such representations intersect with broader socioeconomic and national identity formations vis-à-vis productions of space. As in the following sections in the Element on Taiwan Pride and the Hong Kong Gay Games, this approach nuances homonationalist critiques of Pride by highlighting the emergent and complex ways in which LGBTQIA+ identities are constructed and performed within democratically ambivalent and socially conservative contexts (Webb, 2022). Ultimately, this analysis underscores the performative and political potential of stances and signs to create spaces for alternative discourses and practices that contrasts with Euro-American models of Pride (Jaffe, 2009; Conway, 2023; Go, 2024).

3.2 Methodological Considerations

The research methodology in this section follows an ethnographic approach to the LL (Gorter, 2019). Data was collected during the afternoon program of the 2023 MM Pride march, held on June 24, 2023, at the Circuit Grounds in North-West Makati City. From 12:00 pm to 5:00 pm, I assumed a dual role as both participant and observer, actively engaging with the event while simultaneously adopting an observer's perspective. This approach allowed me to both share in the experiences of MM Pride participants and observe the spatialization processes as they unfolded during the event (Lou, 2017). To facilitate data collection, I used a camera phone to capture a total of 482 photographs, documenting various signs in the LL. Photographs were taken at different segments of the venue and at multiple time points throughout the event. My aim was to understand how public signs and their distribution throughout MM Pride contribute to the creation of a space for LGBTQIA+ celebration and activism. My approach to MM Pride is influenced by my long-term ethnographic engagement with the event. My involvement, which includes a PhD project from 2017 to 2019 and consistent participation in MM Pride events – except during the years when the event moved online due to COVID-19 (2020–21) – has provided me with a sense of familiarity with the event's dynamics. This sustained engagement, coupled with the insights gained through my academic research, has significantly shaped the way I orient to the LL of MM Pride 2023. A critical moment in my ethnographic journey occurred during my 2019 fieldwork, where I observed a pronounced division between issues central to LGBTQIA+ identity politics and broader non-LGBTQIA+ concerns, both of which were articulated through the signages in the LL. This observed distinction among discourses forms a crucial backdrop to my current analysis, guiding my interpretation of the visual and textual elements used in the signs. Specifically, I view them as tools for revealing complex and often contradictory narratives about identity, power, and belonging. The next section presents my analysis of the 2023 MM Pride's LL. It examines how the visual and textual elements captured during the event reflect and contribute to the ongoing discourses surrounding LGBTQIA+ identity, activism, and broader social issues.

3.3 Analysis

This analysis of the signs in MM Pride's LL is structured around three key themes. First, it examines how signs express diverse LGBTQIA+ identities. Second, it explores calls for social and political justice, with a focus on labor rights. Finally, it addresses intersectionality and highlights how LGBTQIA+ issues intersect with broader socioeconomic and national concerns. These themes illustrate how global and local discourses in MM Pride constitute an assemblage of diverse perspectives that represent different forms of marginalization within the country.

3.3.1 Visibility and Celebration of LGBTQIA+ Identity

Within the LL of MM Pride, alongside traditional symbols of Pride (e.g., rainbow flags, hearts), a notable prevalence of signs emerges – those which explicitly articulate expressions of sexual and gender identity. These "sexed signs," adorned with imagery and words, serve as conduits for the participants' agency in asserting and celebrating their sexual and gender identities (Milani, 2014). One particular strategy used in the signs is the deployment of lexis that

Pride in Asia

Figure 6 Signs that represent global LGBTQIA+ discourses.

reflect local engagement with global LGBTQIA+ discourses of visibility, tolerance, and diversity.

The first image in Figure 6 (left) presents strategic deployment of textual and visual elements to convey a layer of stances concerning equality for LGBTQIA+ people. The sign featuring the text "fighting for equality" echoes the international LGBTQIA+ movement's ardent pursuit of extending civil rights to all LGBTQIA+ people – this call is further reinforced by other signs within MM Pride that convey the message "LGBTQIA+ rights are human rights." Appearing with this assertion, the concurrent message "Love has no gender" operates in tandem to disentangle the concept of love from heteronormativity. Through this statement, an alternative conceptualization of love is advanced, untethered from traditional gendered norms. Simultaneously, the use of the planetary symbols ♂ (Mars) and ♀ (Venus) that are stereotypically used to refer to men and women in conjunction with the message serves to further make explicit the stancetaker's challenge to heteronormative notions of love. The combination of these modes creates a stance that envisions a broader, more inclusive spectrum of love that transcends conventional boundaries. The stance thus engages international discourse, advocating for equality, while reshaping conceptions of love within the local context. The second image (Figure 6, right) encapsulates "ready-to-wear sexual politics," where the item of clothing serves as a canvas for a direct and unequivocal proclamation: "Love wins" (Milani and Kapa, 2015). This succinct yet potent message emblematizes the ethos of contemporary LGBTQIA+ movements, indexing affects of triumph, resilience, and optimism, and its placement on an article of clothing transforms it into a wearable form of activism, effectively transmitting its message and underlying stance.

Beyond the deployment of discourses centered around notions of love and equality, MM Pride signs also represented explicit stances that convey sexual

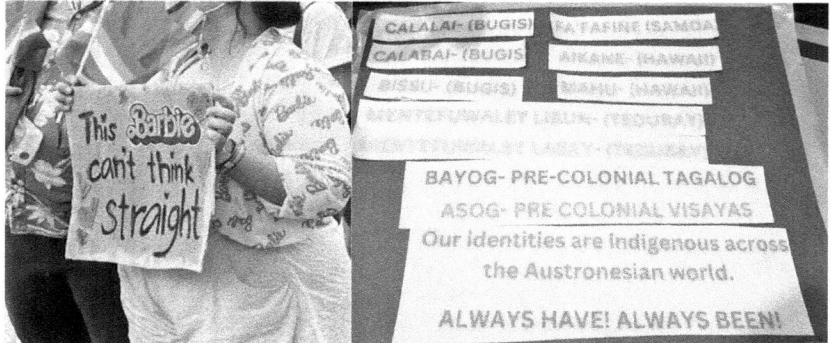

Figure 7 Signs that represent sexual identities.

identifications. One such instance is observed in the first sign (Figure 7, left), bearing the message "This Barbie can't think straight." This sign deploys intertextuality as a tool to convey its message, referencing the online promotional campaign associated with the *Barbie* movie franchise (i.e., the phrase "This Barbie ... ") (Hodges, 2015). This intertextual linkage bridges the mainstream media with LGBTQIA+ representation, which aids in embedding LGBTQIA+ identities through recognizable forms of popular culture. Moreover, by invoking Barbie, a symbol of heteronormative feminine ideals and traditional gender roles and juxtaposing it with the evaluation "can't think straight," this sign disrupts the heterosexual expectations and assumptions. By adopting the name and typography of the Barbie logo, the sign aligns itself with dominant culture – specifically, a commodified notion of heterosexual femininity and womanhood – while simultaneously creating a paradox by acknowledging nonheterosexuality. This discursive move transforms the sign into a tool for disruption, celebrating the deviation from normative expectations.

The second sign (Figure 7, right) enumerates various indigenous gender and sexual identities from Austronesia that transcend the gender binary. In addition to acknowledging and celebrating these indigenous, nonbinary identities, the sign also presents a reminder that these identities are not only rooted in history but an inherent part of the cultural matrix of their respective localities. By doing so, the sign endeavors to decolonize LGBTQIA+ activism, emphasizing the significance of acknowledging and honoring indigenous identities that have often been overshadowed by hegemonic sexual categorizations (Sarce, 2023). Paralleling the case of *kathoey*ness in the Thai protests in the previous section by Pavadee, by identifying these indigenous designations, the signs challenge the limitations of LGBTQIA+ categorization while emphasizing the enduring nature of indigenous categories (i.e., "Always have! Always been!").

Rather than isolating these local identities from LGBTQIA+ categories, the deliberate use of rainbow colors visually unifies and creates a sense of community, while preserving the specificities of these indigenous designations.

3.3.2 Representation of Local Issues

Integrating local issues is another recurrent thematic element within the LL. The additional focus of MM Pride signs on concerns relevant to the Philippines contributes to constructing MM Pride as a space to represent experiences specific to the local LGBTQIA+ community. These calls for justice are emplaced alongside discourses of sexuality, highlighting that MM Pride is also a platform for civic engagement that is aligned with the unique cultural, social, and political context of the Filipino LGBTQIA+ individuals. The signs at MM Pride engage in a dialectical tension, critiquing state and capitalist policies that marginalize local LGBTQIA+ communities while also reproducing their logics (Conway, 2023).

The first image in Figure 8 (top-left) conveys a demand for a higher minimum wage. The sign presents an imperative in Taglish (i.e., English

Figure 8 Signs that present socioeconomic calls.

noun "now" and the Tagalog adverb "na" (trans. "already"). This translingual strategy not only is emphatic but also invokes a sense of urgency, underscoring the dire need for increased wages. This call resonates within the broader societal context, particularly in light of escalating inflation that adversely affects everyday citizens. Meanwhile, the second sign (Figure 8, top-right) conveys a demand for the creation of a magna carta for BPO (business process outsourcing) workers. The demand refers to House Bill No. 8189, or the proposed BPO Workers Welfare & Protection Bill, that aims to institutionalize fair labor practices and enhanced benefits for BPO employees in the country (Cruz, 2023). The call coincides with growing concerns surrounding the workers' rights and exploitative working conditions in the BPO industry and so the call for a legal framework aims to secure the rights of BPO workers. Additionally, the use of a QR code in the sign functions as a bridge between the physical sign and digital spaces, offering viewers an interactive gateway to further information about the magna carta for BPO workers and leveraging the capacity of discourses to move between offline and online landscapes to gather public support (Blommaert, 2019). Lastly, the text, "fuck u Marcos" etched onto a hand-painted cardboard sign encapsulates a potent and assertive stance against the president, Ferdinand Marcos Jr. (Figure 8, bottom). The deliberate use of the expletive "fuck" forcefully conveys a negative assessment of the political figure, President Ferdinand Marcos Jr. Functioning as a linguistic marker of frustration and dissent, it positions the message as a form of protest against Marcos and his administration. Moreover, the sign's physical attributes also contribute to its impact. Its hand-painted quality suggests authenticity and personal investment, while the simple cardboard material aligns with the DIY ethos often associated with grassroots activism. This raw aesthetic emphasizes the unfiltered nature of the sentiment and underscores the accessibility of protest, demonstrating that powerful statements can be made with minimal resources.

In addition to divergence in terms of subject matter, visually the signs are distinguished for not using colors and symbols that index the LGBTQIA+ community, thereby opting for a deliberate departure from the conventional aesthetic associated with Pride events. This visual departure serves as a strategic choice, highlighting participants' intent to foreground social and political issues amidst other signs that focus on LGBTQIA+ representation. The absence of typical LGBTQIA+ symbols challenges participants within the LL to reframe their perception of Pride as a platform that not only advocates for sexual identities but also makes sociopolitical statements, ultimately underscoring the multifaceted nature of MM Pride.

3.3.3 Intersectional Calls

The incorporation of intersectional messages within MM Pride introduces a new dimension to the LL, showing explicit connections between matters of sexuality and urgent social and political challenges specific to the Philippines. While the signs discussed in the previous section can be interpreted as embodying intersectionality through the depicted issues, such as the well-being of BPO workers – where an increasing number of LGBTQIA+ individuals are employed despite the absence of official statistics (e.g., gay men in call centers; Salonga, 2015) – and through their emplacement with LGBTQIA+-focused signs within the physical environment, the signs under this theme establish direct associations between LGBTQIA+ identities and wider societal concerns through both linguistic and visual strategies. This alignment reflects a conscious effort among participants to bridge the gap between LGBTQIA+ advocacy and other forms of injustices, unveiling how the LL becomes a dynamic canvas to foreground how different forms of oppression figure in experiences of marginalization of MM Pride participants.

The sign (Figure 9, top) displaying "Justice for Jennifer Laude" represents a poignant demand within MM Pride and epitomizes the intersections of gender discrimination, challenges faced by individuals from low socioeconomic backgrounds, and the broader implications of the long-standing US military presence in the Philippines. Jennifer Laude was a trans woman and sex worker who tragically fell victim to a hate crime committed by an American soldier who was participating in joint military exercises in the country. Laude's case was historic as it was the first time a US soldier was convicted for committing harm against a Filipino (Valmores-Salinas, 2020). However, the perpetrator was eventually pardoned by former president Rodrigo Duterte, resulting in his release. The visuality of the sign (i.e., colors of the trans flag), combined with an understanding of the intertextual context, highlights Jennifer's gender identity as a trans woman and her positionality vis-à-vis various forms of oppression (for example, her status as a sex worker underscores the socioeconomic limitations faced by many trans women in the Philippines, and her tragic fate and the subsequent release of her perpetrator shed light on broader implications linked to the US military presence in the Philippines). The stancetaker's demand for "justice" transcends individual accountability, extending to larger structures of power that foster an environment in which trans women are vulnerable to violence.

The second image (Figure 9, bottom-left) showcases a sign bearing the message "Mindanaoan Deaf LGBTQIA+ Pride." This visual statement significantly contributes to the LL by foregrounding often overlooked identities within

Figure 9 Signs that present intersectional calls.

the local LGBTQIA+ community. It explicitly asserts a dual identity: being both "Mindanaoan" and part of the LGBTQIA+ community. By doing so, the sign challenges the dominant narrative of LGBTQIA+ experiences centered in urban areas, giving visibility to regional identities. Moreover, the inclusion of "Deaf" expands the representation of marginalized groups within the LGBTQIA+ community. The third image (Figure 9, bottom-right) depicts a shirt displaying the text "safe spaces. higher wages. human rights," utilizing rainbow colors and varying font sizes. This clothing item presupposes the interconnectedness of numerous forms of oppression that impact different marginalized groups, thereby constituting an intersectional call. Firstly, the message incorporates key phrases frequently found in LGBTQIA+ activism, such as "safe space" and "human rights," which are combined with a demand for higher wages. The presence of these phrases, coupled with the use of rainbow colors, contributes to a multimodal alignment that indexes LGBTQIA+ individuals who face socio-economic disadvantage. Notably, the varied text sizes establish visual hierarchies that potentially suggest the prioritization of material needs and rights over safe spaces, introducing a layer of ambiguity. In interweaving these diverse concerns, the shirt prominently showcases less privileged LGBTQIA+ community members, echoing the way the LL at MM Pride functions as a platform for advocating against multifaceted injustices. The distinct intersectional calls unveil the intricate network of sociopolitical dynamics that intersect with gender and sexual identity, underscoring the necessity for comprehensive changes in the government.

The signs that convey intersectional concerns play a pivotal role in strengthening the identity politics and sociopolitical calls within MM Pride, fostering a more comprehensive and inclusive platform for LGBTQIA+ advocacy. These signs that embrace intersectionality demonstrate the ongoing evolution of MM Pride. This evolution is marked by a widening scope that not only encompasses sexuality but also incorporates socioeconomic class, regional differences, and dis/abilities. Moreover, these types of signs counteract the possibilities of intersectional invisibility within MM Pride by acknowledging the diverse range of experiences within the community (Purdie-Vaughns and Eibach, 2008). Equally as important, the convergence of identity politics and more local concerns may lead to forms of intersectional solidarity among LGBTQIA+ people within the immediate vicinity of MM Pride and beyond, creating awareness and distress over the oppression of those who are considered "other" even within LGBTQIA+ community itself (Einwohner et al., 2021).

3.4 Discussion: MM Pride as a Space for Intersectional Activism

This section examined the LL of MM Pride, demonstrating how it functions as a space for both LGBTQIA+ identity expression and broader social activism. While influenced by transnational Pride movements, MM Pride's signs diverge from Euro-American models by addressing local concerns. This intertwining of gender, sexuality, class, citizenship, and other social issues creates a complex "regime of truths." On one hand, the LL of MM Pride affirms and privileges specific groups within the LGBTQIA+ community, yet on the other it obscures the social injustices and precarity faced by marginalized members of this community. At the same time, these signs critique societal structures and power relations, thereby illustrating an attempt to educate and foster solidarity with other marginalized groups. This approach positions Pride as a broader struggle that includes but is not limited to sexual identity.

Central to the politics of MM Pride is a kind of pragmatic approach that attempts to forge solidarities among different marginalized groups through a broader critique of social injustices. The signs emerging from the representational practices create a platform that makes sexual identities visible by reproducing and reworking international LGBTQIA+ discourses and local understandings of sexuality.

Participants seek solidarity with the global LGBTQIA+ community by deploying "globally hypernormalized" LGBTQIA+ discourses while acknowledging indigenous sexual categories (Shirinian and Channell-Justice, 2020, p. 7). In this way, MM Pride both reinforces and challenges prevailing representations of privileged LGBTQIA+ members in relation to notions of social progress. This dynamic reflects an attempt from the local community efforts to reclaim agency and foster a more expansive understanding of LGBTQIA+ experiences within the Philippines, while also managing the hegemony of the international LGBTQIA+ movement. Furthermore, other signs in the LL point to the broader socioeconomic and sociopolitical structures that compound and obscure experiences of inequality and marginalization for the local community. As such, the presence of these signs aids in facilitating an emergent form of intersectional LGBTQIA+ activism. MM Pride employs its signs to challenge systemic inequities, advocating for a just society where all LGBTQIA+ individuals, particularly those most marginalized, are protected and empowered. This resonates with the findings of Lai (2024) and Conway (2023), who note that Filipino migrants participating in Pride celebrations in Hong Kong viewed the fight for equal rights as part of a broader struggle for socioeconomic and political justice.

The assemblage of signs within MM Pride highlights tensions arising from the event's dual nature as both a celebration and a protest. Circulating discourses in the LL emphasize the concerns of a diverse community united by their sexual identity, while also underscoring the importance of situating these identities within other "axes of dominance" (Roth 2021, p. 10). This decentering of international Pride discourses, which largely hinge on sexual identity politics, disrupts the orderliness of categories such as "sexual identity" and "LGBTQIA+ community," which are often understood within the parameters of Western conceptions of sexuality. The LL of MM Pride, instead, proffers a more locally situated and politicized perspective on LGBTQIA+ identity and foregrounds the experiences of individuals frequently excluded from mainstream conceptions of Pride. However, the signs' placement within the stratified organization of Philippine society introduces a degree of ambivalence. For instance, critiques of the government or socioeconomic injustices often elicit negative reactions on social media from some presumably privileged MM Pride participants, who instead favor signs that celebrate LGBTQIA+ identity without engaging with broader social issues. While these tensions between the local and global, and between celebration and protest, remain unresolved, the LL of MM Pride illustrates the "transgressive possibilities" that emerge from the landscaping of intersectional discourses (Hunt and Holmes, 2015, p. 156). MM Pride thus becomes a site where multiple influences converge, creating a space that, while drawing from international LGBTQIA+ discourse, remains attentive to local realities of inequality.

4 Challenging Heteronormativity and Reifying *Tai*-ness: The Linguistic Landscape of Taiwan LGBT+ Pride

Focusing on the slogans and fashion choices in Taiwan LGBT+ Pride, I (Li-Chi), in this section, analyze the linguistic and nonlinguistic patterns that make Taiwan LGBT+ Pride a public space where heteronormativity is challenged, and, most significantly, Taiwanese localness (*tai*-ness) is reified. In Taiwan, a social movement for sexual and gender minorities emerged as early as the 1990s, immediately after the abolition of the martial law (P.-H. Lee, 2017). P.-H. Lee further argues that the revival of conservatism in Taiwan, which combines Confucianism and Christianity, gave rise to a rainbow coalition, which later experienced a series of deterritorializations and reterritorializations. As P.-H. Lee elucidates, the entire coalition cannot be understood as a mere subset of its constituent parts, including neither the movement nor its participants. Its constituent parts must engage with one another in order to generate the properties that characterize it, rather than being understood as a unified, indivisible entity. However, this process of deterritorialization and reterritorialization has transformed the movement into a broader, larger rainbow coalition that promotes the cosmopolitan identity of "Taiwaneseness" based on the pursuit of self-determination and self-liberation. Since 2003, Taiwan has celebrated Pride annually with a public parade. The LGBTQIA+ mobilization in the country has been stimulated by electoral reform in 2008, the outbreak of the Sunflower movement in 2014, and the election victory of the Democratic Progressive Party (hereafter DPP) in 2016 (Ho, 2019). As a Pride parade showcases various forms of the expressive system that convey meanings and are used by Pride marchers to construct their sexual identity, my aim is to analyze how LGBTQIA+ Taiwanese articulate their identity in Taiwan LGBT+ Pride. The database consists of 803 photos taken at Taiwan LGBT+ Pride from 2010 to 2020, all taken from the Taiwan Rainbow Civil Action Association's Flickr images.[1]

4.1 Linguistic Landscape Analysis

Slogans can be associated with sexual and gender ideologies, as evidenced by the digital dating profiles of Serbian gay men (Bogetić, 2020). On the other hand, dress and appearance are used to maintain and display lesbian and gay identities (Holliday, 2001), or as key signifiers of gender and sexuality (Skidmore, 1999). Through an LL analysis of the Pride slogans and fashion over

---

[1] I express gratitude to the Taiwan Rainbow Civil Action Association for promptly responding to my inquiry and granting me permission to cite their images for academic use. Their assistance during the writing of this section was also greatly appreciated.

the past decade, I also discuss how Taiwanese Pride marchers construct their local and global identities in the Pride events.

4.2 Challenging Heteronormativity

Heteronormativity helps to explain how heterosexuality is privileged in society, marginalizing sexual minorities (Warner, 1991). It is also linked to the concept of the nation, as those who are not heteronormative are unlikely to receive the same protection from the nation state (Motschenbacher, 2023). However, five strategies are observed to challenge heteronormativity in Taiwan LGBT+ Pride: *the practice of homonormativity, the discursive construction of sexual desire, the struggle against traditional Confucianism, the redefinition of masculinity,* and *the marginalization of heterosexuality.*

4.2.1 The Practice of Homonormativity

The concept of homonormativity was originally defined as the "sexual politics of neoliberalism" (Duggan, 2002, p. 176) and has been used to normalize or mainstream LGBTQIA+ people by adopting the preexisting heteronormative structure. In Wilton Manors, Florida, for example, same-sex sexualities are constructed as the local norm (Motschenbacher, 2020b, 2023). Homonormativity is also practiced in Taiwan LGBT+ Pride. Figures 10–12 illustrate how same-sex couples conform linguistically or visually to traditional gender roles.

In Figures 10 and 11, both the gay and lesbian couples are found to adopt the heteronormative structure of marriage, as manifested in the verbs *hūn* "to get married" (Figure 10, line 1), *qǔ* "to marry" (Figure 11, line 2), and *jià* "to marry" (Figure 11, line 3). In Figure 11, particularly, the two verbs *qǔ* and *jià* are gendered, further reflecting sexist attitudes (Moser, 1997, pp. 18–19). As Moser further discusses, the verb *qǔ* takes the masculine subject and is semantically or functionally similar to verbs with connotations such as "to take," "to get," "to obtain," "to buy," "to win," and so on. In other words, the subject of this verb, a man, is always the recipient of the action intended for him. On the other hand, the verb *jià* takes a woman as its subject and is frequently followed by a man marked in dative case. Although the third-person singular pronoun 她 *tā* "she" assumes a female referent (Figure 11, line 3), the lesbian couple still adopts the binary gender norm in their same-sex marriage. Similar findings are also seen in Li and Lu's (2020) study, according to which Taiwanese gay men and lesbian women who seek romance online are still influenced by heteronormative ideologies, as evidenced in the keywords containing many binary roles.

Figure 10 Taiwan LGBT+ Pride 2012.

Translation

1. 我們想婚了
   wǒmen xiǎng hūn le
   "We are planning to get married."

2. 在一起6年
   zài yìqǐ 6 nián
   "(We) have been in a relationship for six years."

The binary view of gender roles in marriage is also visualized in Pride fashion, as shown in Figure 12.

A Pride parade exhibits how heterosexual space is "queered" and how the spatial aspect of the event is linked to the expression of particular emotions by

Figure 11 Taiwan LGBT+ Pride 2017.

Translation

1. 交往10th
   jiāowǎng 10th
   "The tenth year of our dating."

2. 她很想娶我
   tā hěn xiǎng qǔ wǒ
   "She wants to marry me so bad."

3. 我只好嫁她
   wǒ zhǐhǎo jià tā
   "I have no option but to marry her."

4. 年底美國結婚
   nián dǐ Měiguó jiéhūn
   "(We) are getting married in America at the end of the year."

those involved (Ammaturo, 2016). Therefore, two individuals of the same gender walking in the Pride parade as a married couple can be seen as creating an LGBTQIA+ space in public. Figure 12 illustrates two types of femininity: women with long hair and dressed in a gown and women with short hair wearing a suit or tuxedo. In the Western world, the establishment of gender guidelines can be traced back to the nineteenth century. In their literature review of the

Pride in Asia 39

Figure 12 Taiwan LGBTQIA+ Pride 2014.

men's suit in the nineteenth century, Alfredsson and Augustsson (2017) point out that the so-called men's suit emerged in the late nineteenth and early twentieth centuries. It was characterized by three pieces: an ensemble of a jacket, waistcoat, and pants made in the same or similar fabric for mass production. The three-piece ensemble can also be observed in modern suits and tuxedos worn by men. Conversely, women's attire was crafted in a more elaborate style due to their comparatively lower societal influence relative to men's in the nineteenth century. The opulence observed in women's attire during the nineteenth century is also reflected in the gowns worn by women in contemporary societies. In light of the above, it can be posited that the two types of femininity depicted in Figure 12 exemplify the traditional gender binary of male and female.

4.2.2 The Discursive Construction of Sexual Desire

Sexual desires and practices can be discursively constructed, as seen in the slogans of Taiwan LGBT+ Pride. While these slogans are humorously presented in antithetical parallelism or contain words that rhyme, their aim is to normalize bodily autonomy and to fight against the stigmatization and discrimination of certain sexual fetishes.

In Figures 13–16, lexical items that are associated with sexual behavior, e.g., *kāoqiāng* "to jerk off" (Figure 13, line 1), *dǎpào* "to hook up" (Figure 13,

Figure 13 Taiwan LGBT+ Pride 2012.

Translation

1. 尻槍不要放槍[2]
 kāoqiāng búyào fàngqiāng
 "Jerk off, instead of discarding a tile from which another player calls mahjong."

2. 愛打牌也愛打炮
 ài dǎpái yě ài dǎpào
 "(I am/We are) into mahjong and also into hooking up."

line 2), *gàn* "to fuck" (Figure 14, line 1), and *chōngzhuàng qiánlièxiàn* "to bang the prostate" (Figure 15, line 1), sex products, e.g., *rùnhuáyóu* "lubricant" (Figure 14, line 2), or sexual kinks and fetishes, e.g., puppy play (Figure 16) highlight sexualization. Interestingly, Mowlabocus (2023) has observed that while chemsex, a type of sexual behavior, is antithetical to homonormativity because it is never associated with the "good gays" but with the "evil queer," both chemsex and homonormativity are structured by a neoliberal morality of self-governance, personal responsibility, and individual sovereignty. In other words, sexual autonomy and agency are discursively normalized in Taiwan LGBT+ Pride as a form of active resistance to heteronormative norms about sexual desires.

---

[2] This is a wordplay based on mahjong, a tile-based game commonly played by four players.

Figure 14 Taiwan LGBT+ Pride 2014.

Translation

1. 同志怎麼幹, 不用你來管
   tóngzhì zěnme gàn, búyòng nǐ lái guǎn
   "How a queer fucks is none of your business."

2. 給我潤滑油, 拒絕黑心油[3]
   gěi wǒ rùnhuáyóu, jùjué hēixīnyóu
   "Give me lubricant, and reject using the tainted oil."

4.2.3 The Struggle Against Traditional Confucianism

Confucianism is a Chinese moral philosophy that entrenches gender stratification. While it created a male-dominated patriarchal family structure and imposed conservative rules on women with the "three obediences" and "four virtues," which led to further sexual discrimination and subjugation of Chinese women and girls (Moeller, 2003), it also placed heavy responsibilities on men. In Taiwan LGBT+ Pride, however, a struggle against traditional Confucian masculinity and the principle of reciprocity for gender duality is observed.

Figure 17 shows two contrasting words, *xiàodào* "filial piety" and *chǎndào* "birth canal," which is a wordplay pair based on rhyme. It can be seen as a humorous rejoinder to the criticism that homosexuality prevents a man from producing a male heir to carry on his family name. Indeed, the pro-marriage and

---

[3] This refers to the "gutter oil" scandal in Taiwan in 2014.

Figure 15 Taiwan LGBT+ Pride 2015.

Translation

1. 衝撞前列腺

   chōngzhuàng qiánlièxiàn

   "Bang the prostate."

2. 年齡不設限

   niánlíng bú shèxiàn

   "This should not have age restrictions."

pro-fertility tradition is associated with Confucian masculinity, which holds that a man's failure to find a wife could lead to social disruption (Yu and Nartey, 2021). As Liao (2020) observes, the Christian-led pro-family movement in Taiwan in 2013 used this rhetoric of Confucian apocalypse to wrap "procreation" with "filial piety," which religious activists see as "the foundation of a harmonious social order" (p. 153).[4] In her research, Su (2023) also notes that

---

[4] Although Taiwan legalized same-sex marriage in 2019, the call for legalizing same-sex marriage in 2013 triggered the Christian-led pro-family movement in the same year.

Figure 16 Taiwan LGBT+ Pride 2020.

Translation

1. 主人摸摸頭

   zhǔrén mōmō tóu

   "The owner gives a pat on the head (of the dog)."

2. 狗狗舔趾頭

   gǒugǒu tiǎn zhǐtóu

   "The dog licks its toes."

a mother blogger opposed Taiwan's legalization of same-sex marriage. The blogger presented herself as a loving and sacrificing mother, while also asserting her right to make decisions for her children. This reflects a traditional view of parenthood influenced by Confucianism. Despite this, as Figure 17 shows, filial piety in traditional Confucian values is directly challenged in Taiwan LGBT+ Pride, but in a humorous way.

Additionally, because Confucian societies have a hierarchy of masculinity over femininity, women or daughters are oppressed. This, however, is challenged in Taiwan LGBT+ Pride to promote gender equality.

In lines 1 and 2, *nán* "male" and *nǚ* "female" are used to refer to baby boys and baby girls or the fetal sex, and in lines 3 and 4, body parts are used for the same purpose. As we can see, the slogans in Figure 18 emphasize gender equality and are directed against those parents or grandparents who are desperate for a son or a grandson. Hajndrych and Wu (2022) analyze Taiwanese folk songs published in

Figure 17 Taiwan LGBT+ Pride 2014.

Translation

1. 孝道不能生小孩
 xiàodào bù néng shēng xiǎohái
 "Filial piety cannot produce heirs."

2. 產道才能
 chǎndào cái néng
 "But the birth canal can."

the *Taiwan New People's Newspaper* under Japanese rule and find that a daughter's value to her birth family was less than a crowing rooster or a watchdog, because she would be married off and become part of another family. A son, on the other hand, could produce a male heir to carry on the family name. Although the situation for daughters is much improved in modern Taiwan, older generations influenced by Confucianism still value sons/grandsons more than daughters/granddaughters.

Figure 18 Taiwan LGBT+ Pride 2013.

Translation

1. 生女生男不重要
   shēng nǚ shēng nán bú zhòngyào
   "Giving birth to a girl or boy is not important."

2. 是男是女鬼知道
   shì nán shì nǚ guǐ zhīdào
   "Who the fuck knows the fetal sex?"

3. 有奶有屌是瑰寶
   yǒu nǎi yǒu diǎo shì guībǎo
   "Boobs and dicks are treasures."

4. 平胸陰道一樣好
   píng xiōng yīndào yíyàng hǎo
   "Flat chests and vaginas are equally good."

Interestingly, Chua (2012) and Rowlett and Go (2021) note that forms of "pragmatic resistance" are often adopted in LGBTQIA+ movements in illiberal Asian regions as strategies for LGBTQIA+ people to integrate themselves into the nation by both conforming to and reconfiguring the normative values favored by the government. Since Taiwan is comparatively more liberal and progressive among East Asian countries that are influenced by Confucianism, and since Confucian traditions are linked by Christian-led pro-family activists in Taiwan to their national identity as Chinese (Liao, 2020), this perhaps further

Figure 19 Taiwan LGBT+ Pride 2015.

Translation

1. 女女雙雙
   nǚnǚ shuāngshuāng
   "Lesbians and bisexual (women)."

2. 跨過來
   kuà guòlái
   "Join us."

3. 不哈你的屌
   bù hā nǐde diǎo
   "Not desiring your dick."

4. 拉拉手正好
   lālā shǒu zhènghǎo
   "Lesbians can just join hands."

demonstrates the Taiwanese Pride marchers' attempt to distinguish themselves from LGBTQIA+ Chinese people (Ning, 2018; Chen-Dedman, 2023).

In fact, the struggle against Confucianism is frequently seen in lesbians' slogans and the display of their bodies in Taiwan LGBT+ Pride.

Figure 19 emphasizes women's sexual autonomy, and Figures 20 and 21 emphasize bodily autonomy. As we can see in Figure 19, the genitive form of the second-person singular pronoun *nǐde* "your" (line 3) is used to refer to a man's sexual organ. As noted by Kuo (2002), while this pronoun can be used

Pride in Asia 47

Figure 20 Taiwan LGBT+ Pride 2010.

Translation

1. 我的平胸我決定
   wǒde píng xiōng wǒ juédìng
   "My flat chest, my decision."

2. T的平胸真帥氣
   T-de píng xiōng zhēn shuàiqì
   "The flat chest of a tomboy is cool."

3. 我的ㄋㄟㄋㄟ我決定
   wǒde nēinēi wǒ juédìng
   "My boobs, my decision."

4. 我要我的平胸美學
   wǒ yào wǒde píng xiōng měixué
   "I want my own aesthetics of a flat chest."

to indicate rapport, it is often used for direct confrontation. Clearly, this pronoun is used to challenge men, suggesting that a woman's sexual desire can be satisfied by another woman. Furthermore, in Figures 20 and 21, a woman's bodily autonomy is discursively constructed through the vague use of the first-person singular pronoun *wǒ* "I" or its genitive form *wǒde* "my." As Kitagawa and Lehrer (1990) explain, the vague use of personal pronouns helps a speaker to refer to a specific group of people, and in our case, to refer to any woman who agrees with the slogans. Because the use of the first-person singular pronoun

Figure 21 Taiwan LGBT+ Pride 2016.

Translation
我又肥又辣
wǒ yòu féi yòu là
"I am fat and hot."

expresses the speaker's "personal belief" (Wilson, 1990), and in our case the belief of the lesbian Pride marchers, this pronoun helps any woman who aligns herself with the slogan to assert her bodily autonomy. In other words, a woman no longer needs to dress and adorn herself to please a man, which is against the three obediences and four virtues in Confucianism.

Note also that in Figure 20, two Mandarin phonetic symbols (*zhùyīn fúhào*), ㄋㄟ, are reduplicated to refer to the vernacular form of a woman's breasts in Taiwanese Southern Min. In her analysis of Taiwanese attitudes toward the contextual use of "refined disposition," Su (2008) argues that poor *qìzhí* (disposition) signals a woman's lack of femininity and her nonstandard use of language, and that social evaluation regulates women's ways of speaking. Therefore, this slogan can further be seen as women overturning the way society as a whole expects them to speak.

4.2.4 The Redefinition of Masculinity

In heteronormative, Chinese-speaking societies, a man's lack of masculinity can undermine his humanness, as manifested in many Chinese martial arts films (Hiramoto, 2017). As Puar (2007) argues, "individual agency is legible only as resistance to norms rather than complicity with them, thus equating resistance and agency" (p. 23). Not surprisingly, a new form of masculinity is created in Taiwan LGBT+ Pride to challenge toxic masculinity.

Figure 22 shows this new form of masculinity, i.e., feminine masculinity, as evidenced by the derogatory term, *niángniángqiāng* "sissy boy; sissy-gun" and the verb, *bǎohù* "to protect." While 娘娘-槍 *niángniáng-qiāng* "sissy-gun" is the play

Figure 22 Taiwan LGBT+ Pride 2011.

Translation
1. 男同志別害怕
   nán tóngzhì bié hàipà
   "Do not fear, gay men."

2. SISSY BOY

3. 娘娘槍保護你
   niángniángqiāng bǎohù nǐ
   "The sissy boy will protect you."

on words of 娘娘-腔 *niángniáng-qiāng* "sissy-accent," which is often used in Chinese to refer to an effeminate man in a negative manner, it is used for self-reference to reinforce the sarcasm triggered by the verb, *bǎohù* "to protect." In other words, feminine masculinity is created to challenge toxic masculinity and femmephobia, which can still be found in the gay community. As Eguchi (2009) observes, effeminate gay men are repulsive to some straight-acting gay men, which Bergling (2001) refers to as "sissyphobia." According to Sánchez and Vilain (2012), gay men's masculine consciousness and anti-effeminacy are associated with the negative feelings about their own sexuality. In other words, gay men's "sissyphobia" is perhaps triggered by their "internalized homonegativity."

It is noteworthy that the English counterpart, sissy boy, is used in the same slogan (Figure 22, line 2). A transnational space is thus constructed through code-mixing. Indeed, gay men frequently use English to construct their global and modern identities. Gay Japanese men, for example, use English to construct a cosmopolitan identity (Baudinette, 2018) or to demarcate spaces for those who conform to the *ikanimo-kei* "obviously gay type" lifestyle favored by gay media in Japan (Baudinette, 2017). LGBTQIA+ youth in Delhi also use English to present themselves as knowledgeable sexual moderns (Hall, 2019). This can be explained by the "prestige function" of English associated with its characterological association with globality and modernity (Haarmann, 1989, p. 16).

4.2.5 The Marginalization of Heterosexuality

Although most public spaces, "presuppose (certain) heterosexual identities, relationships, desires and practices as the norm" (Motschenbacher, 2020b, p. 41), Pride parades are nonheteronormative spaces where gay people collectively come out to support each other. In Taiwan, more and more straight allies are joining the celebrations, who are observed to marginalize heterosexuality.

Figure 23 displays a Taiwan Pride marcher holding a banner apologizing for being heterosexual, using the Mandarin apology expression *bàoqiàn* "to be apologetic" (line 2). According to Ruan and Du (2009), *bàoqiàn* is a verb related to mental activities; therefore, it can be modified by an adverb of degree (e.g., *hěn* "very") to emphasize sincerity. Unlike other Mandarin apology expressions, *bàoqiàn* is used to express uneasiness while also conveying a sense of apology. As further noted by Ruan and Du, the use of this apology expression suggests that the offence is not significant. Therefore, the apology in Figure 23 allows straight allies to show their support in a sarcastic way by marginalizing heterosexuality. The target of the sarcasm is the heteronormative Taiwanese society, as many LGBTQIA+ Taiwanese face pressure in a patriarchal society where heterosexuals are the majority.

Pride in Asia

Figure 23 Taiwan LGBTQIA+ Pride 2016.

Translation

1. 身為異男

    shēnwéi yì nán

    "I am a heterosexual man."

2. 我很抱歉

    wǒ hén bàoqiàn

    "I am very apologetic (about being a heterosexual man)."

4.3 Reifying Tai-ness

The linguistic and discursive practices of localness are traditionally considered as deviating from globalization, as they seem to be associated with nonstandard language use (Su, 2011, 2018). Also due to globalization, certain local linguistic forms have become markers of correctness and can be used to index locality (Johnstone, 2010). Four strategies are observed to reify *tai*-ness: *the constructing of dual identities*, *the application of local semiotics*, *the participation in issues of social justice*, and *the use of mockery as shared humor*.

4.3.1 The Construction of Dual Identities

In the data, I observed that many LGBTQIA+ Taiwanese emphasize their dual identities as members of two minority groups. That is, they march at the

Figure 24 Taiwan LGBT+ Pride 2010.

Translation

1. 我是原住民
   wǒ shì yuánzhùmín
   "I am indigenous."

2. 我是同志
   wǒ shì tóngzhì
   "I am queer."

intersection of both LGBTQIA+ and indigenous Taiwanese identities. This can be seen in their slogans and costumes.

In Figures 24 and 25, the dual identities of LGBTQIA+ and indigenous Taiwanese are discursively constructed. In Figure 24, the dual identities are manifested in two assertives, in which the copula *shì* "to be" connects the subject *wǒ* "I" and the two nominal predicates *yuánzhùmín* "indigenous people" and *tóngzhì* "queer." In Figure 25, the dual identities are expressed in a humorous way by a nonindigenous Pride marcher, not only to show support for LGBTQIA+ Taiwanese indigenous people but also to reverse gender and ethnic stereotypes. In contrast, in Figure 26, the Taiwanese indigenous identity is demonstrated through traditional clothing (see also Section 3 for the discussion of indigenous identities and designations in the 2023 Metro Manila Pride march). To summarize, some Pride marchers reify *tai*-ness at the intersection of their ethnic and gender identities.

Pride in Asia

Figure 25 Taiwan LGBT+ Pride 2014.

Translation

1. 我跟原住民喝酒
   wǒ gēn yuánzhùmín hē jiǔ
   "I drink with indigenous people."

2. 我跟原住民打炮
   wǒ gēn yuánzhùmín dǎpào
   "I hook up with indigenous people."

3. 我跟原住民交往
   wǒ gēn yuánzhùmín jiāowǎng
   "I date indigenous people."

4. 我覺得原住民超屌
   wǒ juéde yuánzhùmín chāo diǎo
   "I think indigenous people are wicked."

5. 性別/族群不再刻板
   xìngbié/zúqún bú zài kèbǎn
   "No more gender and ethnic stereotypes."

4.3.2 The Application of Local Semiotics

Taiwanese Pride marchers also use local semiotics that can only be understood by the local people, as can be seen in the way the marchers present their slogans and the way they dress.

54　　　　　　　　　*Language, Gender and Sexuality*

Figure 26 Taiwan LGBT+ Pride 2015.

The *tai*-ness can be seen through humorous expressions of confrontational politics. In Figure 27, the humor of the slogans relies heavily on visual modalities. As we can see, the slogans are presented as Taoist paper talismans – strips of yellow paper on which words written in cinnabar have the power to drive away demons. In line 1, moreover, the Ministry of Justice, the Registered Partnership Act, and legislation based on discrimination are demonized. Because in 2016 the existing Taiwan Civil Code only recognized heterosexual marriage, there was debate about whether the new bill would only legalize same-sex civil partnerships, not marriage, and not opposite-sex civil partnerships, which is discriminatory. While the slogans, presented as Taoist paper talismans, may evoke a hearty laugh and a knowing smile among the in-group members of the Taiwanese society (Chen, 2017), they are not intended for outsiders.

As in many Pride parades, there were many festive elements, with some participants wearing very campy costumes – carnivalesque costumes that are

Figure 27 Taiwan LGBT+ Pride 2016.

Translation

1. 法務部、同性伴侶法、隔離立法退散
   fǎwùbù, tóngxìng bànlǚ fǎ, gélí lìfǎ tuìsàn
   "The Ministry of Justice, Same-Sex Partnership Act, and legislation based on discrimination, back off."

2. 恐同歧視退散
   kǒngtóng qíshì tuìsàn
   "Homophobic discrimination, back off."

very sexy, colorful, and extravagant. But there were also participants who dressed more casually. As Santino (2011) observes, Pride parades are "ludic, festive, or carnivalesque" events that aim to bring about "a change or transformation in society" (p. 67). Local semiotics can also be observed in the costumes which marchers wear to the festivities. In the data, I observe that many Pride marchers are dressed as ancient figures of Chinese folk religion to reify *tai*-ness.

In Figures 28 and 29, the marchers were dressed as ancient Chinese figures that are still popular in Taiwan. In Figure 28, for example, two marchers were dressed in white and black as two deities in Chinese folk religion responsible for guarding the spirits of the deceased in the underworld, known in Taiwan as Qiye Baye "Seventh and Eighth Masters," or in China as Heibai Wuchang "Black and White Impermanence." The marcher on the right was dressed in red as Zhong

Figure 28 Taiwan LGBT+ Pride 2011.

Kui, traditionally known as the vanquisher of ghosts and evil beings. Although the three figures are from China, they are worshiped in temples and shrines in Taiwan and have become local gods. In Figure 29, the marcher was also dressed as Prince Nezha, a protective deity in Chinese folk religion who is also known as the Marshal of the Central Altar or as the Third Prince in Taiwan. Interestingly, the marcher's costume and the rainbow flag interact to signal the harmony between Taiwanese localism and global queerness. Although the Pride marchers were dressed as figures from Chinese folk religion, their costumes show that Taiwan is a melting pot of cultures. More specifically, Taiwan's diversity, as reflected in its multilingual, multiethnic, and multicultural environment, is how *tai*-ness is embodied.

4.3.3 The Participation in Issues of Social Justice

In common with other research presented across this Element, I also observed that *tai*-ness is reified through the participation of Taiwanese Pride marchers in domestic or international social justice issues. However, this appears to be done to reinforce Taiwan's democracy and also as a form of homonationalism to distinguish Taiwan from China.

Figures 30 and 31 are from Pride 2014, and around the same time the Umbrella Movement emerged during the pro-democracy protests in Hong Kong. The yellow umbrellas in Figure 30 and the slogan in Figure 31

Figure 29 Taiwan LGBT+ Pride 2017.

show the Pride marchers' support for the pro-democracy protests in Hong Kong. This Western-style homonationalism was used by the Pride marchers to differentiate themselves from LGBTQIA+ Chinese in order to reify the local value of Taiwan, as exemplified in Taiwan's "*tongzhi* sovereignty," which according to Chen-Dedman (2023) links the legal rights and sexual citizenship of Taiwanese *tongzhi* (LGBTQIA+ Taiwanese) to the protection of Taiwan's political sovereignty, in response to the "China factor" in Taiwanese society. With respect to the current political climate across the Chinese regions, the contrast with the forms of homonationalism discussed in Ben's research on the Hong Kong Gay Games in Section 5 should be noted here.

Interestingly, Ning (2018) notes that during their ruling period, Taiwan's DPP employed homonationalism to distinguish Taiwan from China, gained international recognition, and presented Taiwan as a civilized country by legalizing

58   *Language, Gender and Sexuality*

Figure 30 Taiwan LGBT+ Pride 2014.

Figure 31 Taiwan LGBT+ Pride 2014.

Translation
1. 撑香港
   chēng Xiānggǎng
   "Supporting Hong Kong's (Umbrella Movement)."
2. 挺同志
   tǐng tóngzhì
   "Supporting LGBTQIA+ people."

Pride in Asia 59

Figure 32 Taiwan LGBT+ Pride 2016.

Translation

1. 小英推成家

   Xiǎoyīng tuī chéngjiā

   "Little Tsai (Ing-Wen) is supporting diverse family formation."

2. 大菊拆我家

   Dàjú chāi wǒ jiā

   "Big (Chen) Chu is pulling down my house."

same-sex marriage. This is exemplified in Figure 32, which highlights homonationalism as a manifestation of the DPP's support for diverse family formation. This slogan, however, sarcastically blames Chen Chu, the former mayor of Kaohsiung who represents the DPP, for urban evictions in the city. According to Holmes (2021), there are members of the LGBTQIA+ community who do not support the presence of uniformed Vancouver Police Department officers at Pride parades because these police officers intend to pinkwash their identities. As the term "pinkwashing" refers to the act of showing support for LGBTQIA+ rights to distract from harmful actions against underprivileged groups, this slogan implies that the legalization of same-sex marriage by the former president of Taiwan, Tsai Ing-Wen, and her DPP government may be seen by some people as an act of pinkwashing the ruling DPP's harm to some underprivileged groups. This echoes Kong's (2023) observation that Taiwan's incorporative homonationalism has its own limitations.

4.3.4 The Use of Mockery as Shared Humor

Chen (2022, 2023) observes that humor helps gay Taiwanese men to voice themselves and build in-group solidarity, and how they interact through humor and teasing reveals how they construct their queer identities. In Taiwan LGBT+ Pride, mockery is often used as shared humor.

As shown in Figure 33, humor is utilized as a means to criticize organizations (or individuals) in Taiwan who are unfriendly toward the LGBTQIA+ community. Specifically, the Family Guardian Coalition (Hùjiāméng), which is composed of various religious groups that oppose same-sex marriage legislation, is mocked in a humorous manner. While an "x" is perhaps used to protect the confidentiality of the Family Guardian Coalition, the LGBTQIA+ community in Taiwan is aware of the targeted group. The substitution of "x" for "hù" in order to maintain confidentiality (i.e., *x-jiāméng*) may serve to strengthen in-group solidarity, as this practice assumes that all members of the Taiwanese

Figure 33 Taiwan LGBT+ Pride 2015.

Translation
希望有一天出櫃也能像x家盟發廢文一樣簡單
xīwàng yǒuyìtiān chūguì yě néng xiàng x-jiāméng fā fèiwén yíyàng jiǎndān
"Hoping that one day coming out would be as easy as shitposting by the Family Guardian Coalition."

LGBTQIA+ community should be aware of who is making it difficult for individuals to come out in the country. Furthermore, the use of popular internet slang (e.g., *fǎ fèiwén* "shitposting") to describe the Family Guardian Coalition's opposition to the same-sex marriage bill on social media is concerning. By comparing "coming out" with "shitposting," this slogan uses mockery as shared humor. This can only be appreciated by the Taiwanese LGBTQIA+ community, who are in a constant struggle for gender equality against the Family Guardian Coalition.

4.4 Conclusion

Ben-Rafael's (2009) four structuration principles associated with linguistic landscapes are significant in the landscape of Taiwan LGBT+ Pride. As we can see, the Pride marchers sought to differentiate themselves from others, often by challenging the heteronormative norms of Taiwanese society. The values and preferences of the LGBTQIA+ community are embodied and reinforced in Taiwan LGBT+ Pride. Various linguistic and visual resources are used to challenge heteronormativity and reify Taiwan's localness. The Pride marchers also attempt to reverse the asymmetrical power relations in heteronormative society.

Major events in Taiwan and around the world from 2010 to 2020 could be observed in the slogans and fashions of Taiwan LGBT+ Pride, such as the "gutter oil" scandal and the sit-in street protests in Hong Kong in 2014, the debate on whether to abolish Article 227 of the Criminal Law in 2015,[5] the urban evictions in Kaohsiung and the controversy over the Amendments to the Civil Code and the Same-Sex Partnership Act by the Taiwanese Ministry of Justice in 2016, the controversy over the promotion of gender equality education in schools in 2017, and the multi-question referendum (focusing on same-sex marriage rights and LGBTQIA+-inclusive education in schools) in 2018. In addition, there are always enemies to target, and the attack is presented in a multimodal and humorous way to attract attention (see also Section 3 for the discussion on incorporating intersectional messages into the 2023 Metro Manila Pride march).

In sum, Taiwan LGBT+ Pride can be viewed as a new way to encourage change in Taiwanese society, which also provides a venue for LGBTQIA+ Taiwanese to communicate with the heterosexual majority or their opponents and to celebrate Taiwan's new human rights achievement. Additionally, the LL of Taiwan LGBT+ Pride I have analyzed in this section further highlights the

---

[5] Under Article 227, one having sex with youths aged between fourteen and sixteen is a crime punishable with up to seven years in prison.

particularities and peculiarities of Asian Pride movements, illustrating the significance of "localness" and the utilization of specific linguistic and visual resources to disseminate the message of LGBTQIA+ solidarity, equality, and legitimacy across the region.

5 "Asia's World City" as Homotopia? Surveying Tensions in the Linguistic Landscape of the Hong Kong Gay Games

In this final section, I (Ben) present research I have conducted on the Hong Kong Gay Games, in my capacity as both a scholar and a volunteer for the event. In doing so, my aim to is to relocalize theoretical questions (homonationalism, homotopia) that have informed research into Pride events in Western contexts, as well as to complement and expand upon the other sections of this Element by providing an analysis of the semiotic/discursive construction of place vis-à-vis the mediatized LL of the Gay Games. Furthermore, in departing from the on-site LL investigations represented in the preceding sections of this Element, my research on the Gay Games draws attention to the polysemous character of Asian Pride events, especially considering the recent impacts of heightened securitization in the Hong Kong context, their representations in the news media, and actions taken by the event organizers in response.

The Gay Games is a major sporting and cultural event with roots in Western LGBTQIA+ community politics and expressions of Pride. Founded by Tom Waddell, a former US Olympian, the first event took place in San Francisco in 1982. The vision for these inaugural games was for athletes to take part in a nonhomophobic sporting environment and, moreover, to counter stigmatizing stereotypes of the LGBTQIA+ community. The emphasis of the first Gay Games was on inclusivity, equality, and community building (Symons, 2010; Davidson, 2013), a mission that has continued to define all subsequent games. However, since the San Francisco Games, the event has grown significantly in size and scope, with multimillion-dollar budgets used to stage a massive athletic and cultural spectacle that attracts thousands of participants and spectators from all over the world. Although the Gay Games has been held every four years in various cities, to date these had all been in the West, for example in North America, Europe, and Australia, giving rise to criticisms that the games may potentially exclude those who are neither White nor Western (Waitt, 2006; Davidson, 2013). It seems that, partially in response to such criticisms, Gay Games 11 was chosen to be held for the first time in Asia, with representatives from the Chinese Special Administrative Region of Hong Kong (HK SAR) securing the winning bid to host the event in 2022 (postponed to 2023 for pandemic-related reasons).

Figure 34 Gay Games 11 logo.

The logo for the Hong Kong Games (Figure 34) depicts a Chinese *sampan*, a type of traditional sailing vessel associated with the iconic Victoria Harbour, its customary red sail replaced in this design by a rainbow sail, the symbol of the LGBTQIA+ movement. In this way, the logo functions semiotically to represent the crossing of the Gay Games brand into new spaces, as it travels from West to East.

This crossing is also captured in the initial promotional video from the Hong Kong Games' organizers where the physical and cultural diversity of the city, and its sporting communities and people, are visually and metaphorically linked together via a shooting rainbow ribbon of light to introduce the games' slogan – unity in diversity (Gay Games 11 Hong Kong 2023, 2020). Statements on the Gay Games website, such as, "Hong Kong is a city of so many diverse cultures, a treasure chest of traditions, a melting pot of languages and home to a population of 7+ million proud people" (gghk2022.com/en/welcome-to-gghk) fashion an enduring image of diversity and inclusion, intertextually and interdiscursively drawing on the "Asia's World City" brand, promoted by the Hong Kong Tourism Board. Importantly however, the promotional website also establishes the event's significance via its sociopolitical potentials, through constructions of Asia as, "a region where there is an ongoing struggle to overcome homophobia and acceptance" (gghk2022.com/en/welcome-to-gghk). While there is no explicit criticism of either Hong Kong or other Asian governmental policies per se, the event is attributed some form of purpose as an opportunity to publicly counter ("overcome") prejudices in the region.

Despite this image of Hong Kong, as represented in the Gay Games promotional materials, over the past few years the territory's citizens have experienced unprecedented social and political upheavals, with a severe crackdown on the operations of pro-democracy leaders and other civil societies; a crackdown that has drawn strong condemnation from Western democracies. Compounding these events, zero-COVID policies resulted in a three-year-long withdrawal of Hong Kong from the world, a situation from which, at the time of writing, the city is only just beginning to recover. As a result, the organizers of the Gay Games have seen their efforts in promoting and staging this international mass-scale Pride event caught up in a more recent narrative of Hong Kong, emerging from and imbricated in current geopolitical formations of "China vs. the West." In the light of these broader tensions, in this section I set out to examine how the staging of the Hong Kong Gay Games, an event modeled on Western progressive sociopolitical movements, became entangled in and responded to this rapidly changing narrative by taking as my analytical focus the discursive production of place vis-à-vis the games. The data consists of a small corpus of news stories and opinion articles gathered from the local mainstream English language news media and published across a six-year period (from 2017 to 2022), which corresponds to the beginning trajectory of the games. This trajectory spans the following events: from securing the winning bid, to the impacts of extenuating circumstances: the pandemic and the imposition of a National Security Law in response to violent protests in the city, moving to a point where the organizers had to make significant logistical and discursive adjustments, in order to successfully promote and "safely" hold the event in November 2023. Accordingly, it is their socio-pragmatic responses to these various contingencies that become significant here.

While the other Asian Pride events examined in this Element can be considered as public manifestations of locally emergent social movements, the staging of the Gay Games is more closely linked to place via the capitalization of a particular image of the host city (and by extension the nation) in order to attract participants to the event (not unlike the more commercial Pride events held in the West). As such, the news articles and opinion pieces I have examined here aid in "the textual mediation or the discursive construction of place" (Jaworski and Thurlow, 2010, p. 1), revealing how the Gay Games is positioned as (re)shaping, or even disrupting, both local and global images of Hong Kong. In other words, the media coverage of the Gay Games can be analyzed in terms of its spatializing potentials across the period in question, constituting in this way a "turbulent" LL of Pride in Hong Kong as the city emerges in the new "post-security law" and "post-COVID" era. In this respect, the relationship between the state, and its institutions, and (homo)sexualities is seen as constituting an integral component to the staging and promotion of the games. Such an understanding affords us with the opportunity in this Element to again critically engage with notions of homonationalism concerning Asian Pride events (Lazar, 2017; Rowlett and Go, 2021, 2024). However, in contrast to Taiwan's version of incorporative homonationalism discussed by Li-Chi in Section 4, I aim to explore how a reading of homonationalism in post-security law Hong Kong may now be more closely related to Milani and Levon's (2019) concept of "homotopia" – "an inherently ambivalent place that is both utopian and dystopian" (p. 607). As such, and in light of the tensions imbricated in the buildup to the Hong Kong Gay Games, I end this section with a consideration of homotopia as a potentially useful theoretical basis in interpreting the discursive production of place linked to forms of Asian LGBTQIA+ pride/homonationalism.

5.1 Media Representations of the Hong Kong Gay Games

The analysis focuses on a survey of articles (n=47), including news stories and opinion pieces, published about the event by local English language news media. Most of these articles (44) are taken from the *South China Morning Post* (SCMP), a privately owned daily print and online newspaper that has one of the widest distributions and readerships of traditional news media in English in Hong Kong. Other articles (2) are from *China Daily* (a Chinese state-owned English language newspaper) and (1) the *Hong Kong Free Press* (an independent local English language online news service). Despite online searches for mainstream news media written in Chinese using relevant keywords, the relative scarcity of coverage at the time of this search revealed that the event was being reported on much more widely in the local mainstream English language press via not only news articles but also opinion pieces and letters to the editor. The limitations of this survey, restricted here to media coverage predominantly in one mainstream English newspaper, therefore need to be acknowledged. However, these limitations can also be regarded as instructive, implying in this way that the Gay Games, as an event, may only be pertinent to the local and international (i.e., cosmopolitan) English-speaking community. In addition, the almost exclusive use of English on the (ostensibly) multilingual Gay Games promotional website should also be noted. Each article was manually coded according to the identification of common themes across the data set:

- LGBTQIA+ rights in Hong Kong (and Asia)
- Championing diversity and inclusion
- Images of Hong Kong with relation to the games
- Economic benefits of the games
- Controversies (criticisms of the Gay Games, homophobia)
- Impacts of COVID restrictions on the games

Table 1 shows the number of articles published between 2017 and 2022, together with the number of articles corresponding to each theme in each year.

Table 1 Key themes emerging from local English news media publications on the Gay Games Hong Kong

	2017 (6)	2018 (4)	2019 (2)	2020 (1)	2021 (26)	2022 (8)
LGBTQIA+ rights in Hong Kong (and Asia)	6	2	0	0	1	1
Championing diversity and inclusion	0	2	1	1	15	3
Images of Hong Kong with relation to the games	6	2	2	1	21	3
Economic benefits of the games	2	1	0	0	8	1
Controversies (Criticism of the Gay Games, homophobia)	0	0	0	0	20	7
Impacts of COVID restrictions on the games	0	0	0	1	4	3

Broadly speaking, the occurrence (and recurrence) of each theme corresponds to incidents, or newsworthy events, related to the Gay Games that arose during the period in question. For example, all six articles published in 2017, soon after it was announced that Hong Kong had secured the winning bid to host the event, addressed the benefits that the Gay Games would potentially have on increasing LGBTQIA+ rights in Hong Kong. Two representative headlines from this news cycle thus read:

(a) "Calls for Hong Kong to *better protect LGBT rights* as city wins bid to host 2022 Gay Games."
(D. Lee, 2017; emphasis added)
(b) "The Gay Games is *Hong Kong's moment to show the city's inclusivity.* Are we ready?"
(Guy, 2017; emphasis added)

The language used in these headlines points to desirable futures, where the "protection" of LGBTQIA+ rights and inclusivity are foregrounded as commensurate with the aims and spirit of the Gay Games, and LGBTQIA+ pride more generally. These headlines should also be read in the context of nascent victories gained by Hong Kong LGBTQIA+ activists in preceding years, where courts had ruled in favor of dependent visas and equal tax assessments for same-sex married couples, although it must be noted that these only apply to non-Chinese nationals as same-sex marriage for Chinese couples remains illegal in Hong Kong. It is important also to make clear that, despite these small victories in the final court of appeal, the Hong Kong Legislative Council (Legco) at the time was (and indeed remains) encumbered by pro-establishment politicians who sought to block any progressive laws related to issues of sexual rights (Kong, 2019).

Although, as Kong (2019, p. 1916) points out, Hong Kong Pride has more generally been "based not on the triumph of political rights but on queer cultural achievement," a prominent discourse emerges from these 2017 media reports centring on the opportunity the Gay Games presents for the city to increase its international standing vis-à-vis LGBTQIA+ rights legislation. As such, and specifically with relation to the discursive production of place, a thematic thread addressing the need to promote a progressive image of Hong Kong to a global audience features across the data set as a whole. For instance, the SCMP opinion piece associated with headline (b) states:

"Without government support that is open and enthusiastic, the *antipathy, grudging and almost disapproving response* will grow into a *global public relations disaster* for Hong Kong" (Guy, 2017; emphasis added).

Referencing the reaction ("antipathy, grudging, and almost disapproving") of the government to the news of the winning bid, with then chief executive Carrie Lam reported as merely "noting" the event (Guy, 2017), the writer uses emotive terms such as "disaster" to frame the potentially missed opportunity for a global public relations coup. The economic benefits of the event are similarly fore-grounded throughout the articles, with the above opinion piece citing the USD 52 million generated by the Gay Games held in 2014 in Cleveland, Ohio. After a lull in coverage over the ensuing two years (2018–20) as the story of the games coming to Hong Kong became subsumed by immediate and pressing events taking place in Hong Kong (the Anti-Extradition Law protests and subsequent introduction of the National Security Law (NSL), and the developing COVID-19 pandemic), there was a sudden increase in local English-language reporting on the games in 2021 with twenty-six articles published in that year alone. The main reason for this brief media storm relates to an incident in June 2021 when the organizing committee sought the assistance of a member of Legco to secure government venues for the event. On bringing this request to the council, the ensuing debate, as recorded in media reports, firmly established the level of resistance to the event from several pro-establishment members of Legco. Examples of such statements are:

(a) "*It is your business what you do in your own room*, but if you go out and do it in public, *it's disgraceful*," said Ho [Legco member Junius Ho]. "The point is simple, the officials should not get involved in this, it's the civil society's business if they want to do it, it's wrong [for the government] to throw money into this, and *I don't want to earn this type of dirty money*, it doesn't matter if we earn the HK$1 billion." (Ng, 2021; emphasis added)

(b) "On the surface, it is about *equal opportunities*, it is about *inclusion*. But it does not take a genius to figure out it is *a wolf in sheep's clothing*," citing article 23 of the mainland's NSL which states that *the country should carry forward the traditional culture of the Chinese people and guard against and resist the impact of harmful culture*." (Ng, 2021; emphasis added)

(c) "The government should not take it lightly. The organisers are not a well-organised body. *No one can tell for sure what the participants will wear, what flags they will carry when they are in Hong Kong*." (Ng, 2021; emphasis added)

The image of Hong Kong constructed here is very different from the image constructed back in 2017, when the games was seen as not only being a public relations opportunity for the city, together with the economic benefits it would bring, but also spearheading the ongoing march toward legislation that would better protect the rights of the LGBTQIA+ community in the city. In contrast to the hopes expressed then, the inflammatory rhetoric, characterized by homophobic language in (a) such as "it is your business what you do in your own room"; "it's disgraceful"; and "I don't want to earn this type of dirty money" buttresses a position where the fight for "equal opportunities" and "inclusion" is analogous to subterfuge – "a wolf in sheep's clothing" – as stated in extract (b). In other words, the position taken in these statements equates the Gay Games with threats to national security. Moreover, national security, as represented in these statements, is interpreted as the need to resist "harmful culture"; a discursive production of place that foregrounds the preservation of traditional Chinese (heteronormative) culture and values in the face of "malign" outside influences (see also Ng and Li, 2022). Evidently, such a position is reliant on prevalent and current discourses of national security in the region, feeding off the establishment of an NSL in Hong Kong by the central government in response to violent mass pro-democracy protests in 2019. The Gay Games is therefore ascribed in these statements with an indexical potential that ranges from perversion – "it's your business what you do in your own room" – to subversion – "the government should not take it lightly." Its subversive potential is underscored in statement (c) where the participants in the event are positioned as likely transgressors who will wear prohibited symbols on their clothes or carry outlawed flags. While the clothing and flags are not specified, it can be understood that they may be representative of disputed territories in the region, as evidenced in the news that one of these territories will not be sending any participants to the games – "Taiwan won't attend Hong Kong's Gay Games fearing security law" (Wang and Taylor, 2021).

With this striking discursive shift in constructions and representations of the Hong Kong Gay Games, a febrile debate was sustained in the local English language press on this topic throughout 2021, typified by visceral reactions to the homophobic bluster of the lawmakers cited above, where twenty out of twenty-six articles debated the issue (Table 1). Representative headlines are:

(a) "*Reject bigotry* and get behind Hong Kong's Gay Games." (SCMP Editorial, 2021; emphasis added)
(b) "Hong Kong Gay Games: *prejudice and hatred in Legco fall foul of Beijing's desire for social harmony*." (Wu, 2021; emphasis added)
(c) "*Hong Kong supports Gay Games and LGBT rights*, but Legco does not reflect that." (Faulkner 2021; emphasis added)

With headlines calling for a rejection of bigotry (a) and pointing out the prejudice and hatred in Legco (b), the discursive (re)construction of Hong Kong as a place where the LGBTQIA+ rights are supported by the people (c) despite the position of Legco members intersects with this debate (as represented in twenty-one articles on the theme of Hong Kong's image out of the twenty-six). The opinion piece associated with headline (b) even appears to engage in a form of "reverse discourse" (Foucault, 1990) by emphasizing the damage that homophobic and divisive attitudes from the government will have on social cohesion in the city, the implication being that social harmony, as desired by Beijing in its imposition of the NSL, will be impaired in the name of national security. With the chief executive at the time briefly stepping in to offer her support to the Gay Games and lightly admonishing the actions of members of her government (Lau and Cheng, 2021), it appeared that the storm surrounding the games was abating. However, it was also apparent that the discourse impacting the games had irrevocably changed. Any association with national security issues and foreign interference in Hong Kong affairs, if only at this stage insinuated by a few outspoken government representatives, had the potential to bring into question the motivations of the Gay Games organizing committee. Compounding this situation, the government's strict COVID prevention policies during the period in question threatened the very survival of the games, with this issue discussed in four articles that year (Table 1). These policies resulted in a decision by the games umbrella body, the Federation of Gay Games, to move many of the sporting events to Guadalajara, Mexico as cohosts.

It is therefore within this turbulent LL of the Hong Kong Gay Games, seen in the various and often contrasting discursive constructions of place and sexuality in the media between 2017 and 2021, that a clear purpose to the linguistic strategies deployed by the organizing committee in their communications with the media and the public can be detected:

(a) "We understand that there will always be diverse views in Legco, and *we respect our legislators' right to share them*." (Mok, 2021; emphasis added)
(b) "Some have posited that Hong Kong is not yet ready to recognise same-sex marriage. *Let us be very clear here*. Hosting the Gay Games *does not amount to an endorsement of marriage equality*." (Wong, 2021; emphasis added)
(c) "*We are strictly non-partisan and non-political*, and *we ask all participants and visitors to respect and observe local laws and customs* during their stay in Hong Kong." (Wang and Taylor, 2021; emphasis added)
(d) "'The Gay Games is *not an activist event*,' he said. 'There will be arts and culture events, but there will be *no pride parade*, and it is *not a platform to advocate for any particular legislation*.'" (Wang, 2021; emphasis added)

The strategies represented in this selection of statements are rendered through a series of epistemic stances that seek to mitigate the effects of critical or hostile discourse. These range from assertions of "respect," whether this is respecting the right of those with opposing views to share them (a) or asking participants to respect local sensitivities linked to such opposing views ("customs") when participating in the games (c), to disavowals of intentions attributed to the organizing committee by their critics. For example, the strong epistemic stance represented in statement (b) – "Let us be very clear here" – is deployed to counter criticisms that the Gay Games endorses "marriage equality," and therefore, by extension, any form of rights advocacy. This line of defense is sustained via statements in (c) and (d), where modality and negation are used to demarcate the event from previous knowledges and expressions of LGBTQIA+ pride; those which have long been understood as indexing progressive calls for social justice, both globally and regionally. Through this discursive work, the organizing committee therefore position themselves and the event as "strictly non-partisan and non-political," and emphatically state what the Gay Games is *not:* "it is not an activist event"; "there will be no pride parade"; "it is not a platform to advocate for any particular legislation." As a direct response to the accusations of political subversion from establishment members, such statements from the organizing committee are not entirely unexpected, especially when considering, as earlier in this section, that the very survival of the event, ascribed by some as a "threat" to national security, has been placed at stake. In this way, the shift in language strategies is mirrored via thematic developments across the data set, fashioning a regionally and politically sensitive LL of the games, where the prevalence of themes related to LGBTQIA+ rights (equal marriage etc.) and expressions of sexual identity, such as those which predominate in Christian's research on Metro Manila Pride (Section 2), diminishes in favor of more generalist themes of diversity and inclusivity related to social harmony, and an image of Hong Kong that should nurture such harmonizing qualities.

5.2 Discussion: Asia's World City as Homotopia?

In seeking to understand the linguistic and semiotic construction of place with relation to Asian Pride, through mediated representations of the Hong Kong Gay Games, it has become clear that we cannot treat the buildup to this Pride event as separate from both past and currently circulating discourses concerning Hong Kong and its citizens, and its entanglements in evolving regional and global sociopolitical tensions. On the one hand, the games is presented throughout the data in coherence with the government's "Asia's World City" branding: a place of social and cultural diversity and inclusion. Relatedly, the games is attributed political purpose as it has the capacity to enhance this brand, and thus the city's international standing, by spearheading the progress of LGBTQIA+ rights in the region. On the other hand, such representations also mark the ambivalence of the Hong Kong government with respect to harnessing these potential opportunities, implying that the lack of government support for Pride events such as the Gay Games, hinders this progress. As such, discourse of this type may be said to engage with homonationalist (Puar, 2007) inclinations, in that the mutually beneficial relationship between the state and (homo)sexualities is used to frame the discussion of social issues brought about by holding the Gay Games. However, the tensions produced through such representations appear to reaffirm what Kong (2023) has identified as a "weak" version of homonationalism. In other words, this is a version of homonationalism that does not represent a macro-discourse engineered by the state but instead comes from civil society (see also Lazar, 2017), an understanding demonstrated clearly in other sections of this Element, namely in Christian's and Li-Chi's analyzes of Pride Parades in Manila and Taipei. Further complicating top-down readings of homonationalism in this case, the teleological model of Pride, as represented by the Gay Games brand and established in earlier media reports in the data set, is, in fact, ruptured by accusations from establishment figures that attribute LGBTQIA+ movements with subversive potentials. As a result, the Gay Games, and by extension any LGBTQIA+ Pride event in the city, is constructed locally as a risk to national security – a recently circulating discourse impacting and shaping all levels of social life in the city. The ensuing response from the Gay Games organizing committee is therefore characterized by a strategic decoupling of rights-based discourse from the event, circling back to a reliance on the more generalist government-sanctioned brandings of Hong Kong as a safe, harmonious, cosmopolitan, and inclusive world city, despite narratives of recent years that counter such an image.

Mindful of criticisms that have been voiced about the application of homonationalist readings of LGBTQIA+ social movements in Asia and other non-Western contexts, as such applications may only succeed in replicating colonialist ontologies (Ng and Li, 2022), the analysis presented in this section does not seek to establish homonationalist discourse, as commonly understood from a Western perspective with respect to Pride events, as a defining feature of the Hong Kong Gay Games. At the same time however, and in line with Milani and Lazar (2017), the analysis works with the notion of "dialogic entanglements" (p. 311) where theoretical concepts derived from Western contexts may be productively brought into dialogue with what is observable in other contexts. Particularly important in this respect is a focus on the actions of citizens (individuals, communities, organizations, etc.) themselves in their responses to and negotiations with the state, seen here in the tactics of the local Gay Games organizing committee that point to the use of homonationalist discourse from below (Lazar, 2017; Yue and Leung, 2017). It is in this sense, therefore, and in the spirit of dialogic entanglement, where it can be suggested that the turbulent LL of the Hong Kong Gay Games may usefully be interpreted as a discursive construction of place with relation to Milani and Levon's (2019) concept of "homotopia." Milani and Levon offer this concept as a critical response to paradigmatic renderings and rejections of homonationalist theory; a concept that can be directed toward capturing the ambivalences generated by (dis)attachments to places (e.g., nation states) that are seen as being both utopian and dystopian. Their understanding of homotopia is achieved by scrutinizing the "push and pull" (p. 607) experienced by Palestinian men in their relationship(s) with the Israeli state, constructed both as a "gay haven" yet also as a place of oppression. Reworking the Foucauldian concept of heterotopia (Foucault, 1986) to encompass the spatial politics of sexuality, Milani and Levon argue that, like heterotopias, homotopian sites can engender "ambiguous juxtapositions of hegemony and anti-hegemony, normativity and antinormativity" (Milani and Levon, 2019, p. 609). Conceptualizing the politics of sexuality (Pride) with relation to place and space in this way thus provides an analytical entry point toward understanding the often-ambivalent experiences of those who are compelled to operate within contradictory spatializing systems of freedom and repression.

As presented in this section, the discursive constructions of place that emerge from this survey of media reports on the Hong Kong Gay Games tend to appear in contradictory, and therefore ambiguous, ways. The metaphorical push and pull, as described by Milani and Levon, can be discerned in how this international mass-scale LGBTQIA+ event is sanctioned by the Hong Kong government yet is simultaneously marginalized owing to their indifference, seen, for example, in the lack of any state institutional support for the games. Still, the prevailing discourse of the majority of the SCMP opinion articles is characterized by the voicing of public support in Hong Kong for LGBTQIA+ communities and events, thus constructing an image of place that is liberal and inclusive (it should be noted that in a recent survey, 85 percent of Hong Kong citizens agree that same-sex couples should have equal rights to opposite-sex couples, and 60 percent support same-sex marriage [Lau, Loper, and Suen, 2023]). However, this type of discourse is troubled by the amplified voices of a powerful minority who seek to equate any progressive politics (e.g., sexual minority rights) as a threat to national security, thus constructing an image of Hong Kong that aligns with Beijing government narratives of Chinese exceptionalism and moral superiority vis-à-vis what they see as Western hegemony. This study therefore reveals that the organizers of the Gay Games event are caught within this net of conflicting discourses: at once being compelled to advocate for progressive politics *and* advocate for the status quo.

With respect then to the titular question posed in this section on whether Hong Kong, Asia's World City, can be considered as a homotopia, it is necessary in this case to address how homotopias may also generate what Milani and Levon (2019) call "vicious belonging" – "an identitarian project that we argue is characterized by inherent incongruity and irresolvable tensions," (p. 625) as evidenced in the talk of the Palestinian men featured in their analysis. As such, this beginning survey of constructions of place via media reports on the Hong Kong Gay Games is necessarily rather limited, as the data do not foreground aspects of vicious belonging related to peoples' actual lived experiences. However, it can also be said that the push and pull experienced by the event's organizers, as demonstrated in their mediated responses to the hostile discourse levelled at the games, constitutes, in this way at least, a form of vicious belonging, as they navigate their position between and across conflicting discourses of national identity, security, Pride, and social justice. Moreover, as discussed in this section, it is crucial to see this Pride event in the context of past, present, and future discourses related to the "rise of China." Kong's (2023) recent transregional study of young gay men's lived experiences across Hong Kong, Taiwan, and the mainland provides us with ample evidence that these young men may indeed experience forms of vicious belonging as they (de)construct their relationship to the state in their narratives – again, homonationalism from below. As such, Kong's call for greater attention to "homo-transnationalism" (Bacchetta and Haritaworn, 2011), as a way of capturing "the complexity of state-sexuality relationships on a transnational scale," (p. 154) may find synergy with a recognition of homotopias as potentially transnational phenomena, as demonstrated in part by this study of Hong Kong's Gay Games.

It remains to be seen, in my ongoing research on the Hong Kong Gay Games and in interviews with other volunteers, whether assumptions of vicious belonging generated by this reading of Hong Kong as homotopia may, in actuality, be manifested in the perspectives and experiences of those taking part (including other Asian participants). Nevertheless, in concluding this section, and in line with this Element's aims in unravelling the complexities of Asian Pride events in locally sensitive and highly contextualized ways, I suggest that an engagement with, and reworking of established paradigms, such as homonationalism, via not only local but also transregional or transnational understandings may offer productive future avenues of research.

6 Conclusion

By bringing together our research on Asian Pride events in this Element, our aim has been to examine manifestations and expressions of Pride by combining local and transregional perspectives. This is by seeking inspiration from the approaches of queer Asian studies/Asia as method, as we work toward a sociolinguistic understanding of Pride within and across "Asias," accounting for both theoretical commonalities and diversities via a focus on those taking action on the ground. What we have discovered in the process is that an ideology of Pride, as it has travelled across time and space, from Stonewall to the present, from the "West" to the "East," finds not only currency but also latitude and pliability. In other words, the Pride events we examine are not carbon copies of larger and more established events in the West but are distinguished by particular and expressively local calls for, amongst other things, visibility, inclusivity, legitimacy, and change. While we note how these local calls often draw on the ideologies, motivations, and iconographies of Pride as a global phenomenon, it is clear that these undergo various translations in accordance with local priorities and concerns. For example, we see theorizations emerging from our research that address how ideologies of LGBTQIA+ Pride are: (a) mobilized to enhance the broader pro-democracy movement in Thailand; (b) used to forge intersectional alignments between marginalized groups in the Philippines; (c) used politically to shape the reification of Taiwanese identities in distinction to those associated with mainland China; and (d) imbricated in responses to threats emerging from top-down national security drives in Hong Kong.

In order to unpack the sociopolitical currents impacting and shaping expressions of Pride in Asia(s), our research collectively hones in on the semiotic processes that inform the signage, slogans, adornments, and images that are strategized for display and messaging at these events, along with other mediatizations of LGBTQIA+ Pride in public discourse. In this way, the analytical methods used in each section broadly follow the approaches of LL research, but vary in accordance with the specificities of each event. For instance, Pavadee focuses on processes of iconization in the signs, speeches, and activities to establish the emergence of *kathoey*ness as an icon that brings the LGBTQIA+ community together as Thai citizens, whereas Christian uses examples of stancetaking in the LL of Metro Manila Pride as an entry point toward theorizing how intersectional discourse motivates alternative imaginings of Pride. Both Li-Chi and Ben examine how semiotic processes of homonationalism are relevant to the LL of Pride events in Taiwan and Hong Kong respectively, yet find clear divergences between homonationalist inclinations as a strategy of differentiation in terms of national identity in Taiwan, and as a way of responding to recent instabilities, uncertainties, and insecurities faced by the LGBTQIA+ community in Hong Kong.

In all of the events we examined, we therefore see how the semiotic processes that relate nonnormative gender and sexuality to broader social concerns are manifested as sociolinguistic actions, albeit ones that are deployed with relation to the contextual specificities informing each Pride(-like) event via, for instance, references to local politics and the use of in-jokes. However, it is by understanding Asian Pride in terms of sociolinguistic action that we discern a clear transregional response to issues of sexual citizenship. The actions we analyze across each event and locale therefore find a collective relevance and urgency as acts of citizenship (Isin, 2017), a notion that Pavadee theorizes most comprehensively in her section on LGBTQIA+ participation in the Thai pro-democracy movement. The LGBTQIA+ communities whose situated actions form the basis of our research are therefore seen to draw on ideologies of Pride to assert their visibility and legitimacy as citizens through their locally grounded and creative (and often humorous) use of language and imagery, their engagements with the media, and, perhaps most importantly, through their embodied presence in public spaces via Pride events and affirmative actions on the streets and, increasingly, in online spaces.

That said, in using a transregional perspective to bind our various research narratives together in this Element, we have become acutely aware of how divergences and uneven trajectories of Pride characterize the "Asias" we examine. At the time of writing, there is cause for celebration, for example, with the recent enactment of the same-sex marriage law in Thailand, but the situation for some LGBTQIA+ communities in the region remains precarious. This is most ostensibly seen in the crackdown on civil liberties and freedoms of expression, often in the name of national security, that Ben's research on the Hong Kong Gay Games has brought into sharp focus here. Further research on Pride in Asia might therefore begin to engage more fully with sociolinguistic theories related to (in) securitization (Rampton and Charalambous, 2020), especially concerning queer lives and experiences (Levon, 2020; Milani and Levon, 2024). In addition, by foregrounding acts of citizenship through mobilizations of Pride (as we do here), we need to be wary, as Comer (2022) rightly warns, of how Pride movements (and resultant forms of homonationalism, for example) may be promoting neoliberal forms of citizenship that bypass the lived realities of many queer communities in these regions. In this sense, we see a need to more fully explore and account for movements of people across Asian regions and how these movements may intersect with local Pride formations in the LL. For example, recent work by Conway (2023) examines how migrant expressions of Pride in Hong Kong are used as a platform to contest global capitalism; issues which Christian also discusses in his section on MM Pride. Migrant precarities, in this way, are further manifestations of (in)securitization where LGBTQIA+ communities are unevenly structured according to wealth, ethnicity, and gender.

To conclude, and returning once more to the broader aims of queer Asian studies, we expect that future sociolinguistic research on Pride in Asia will continue to find points of "dialogic entanglement" with theorizations and ideologies of Pride across the globe. Yet this research will also maintain its focus on local sensitivities through a grounded approach. In doing so, we can also expect that these sensitivities will aid in our interpretations of how both space/place and gender/sexuality are constructed in often contradictory and ambivalent ways through Pride events in Asian contexts. More importantly, such approaches will also aid in understanding how people use linguistic and semiotic resources to negotiate these contradictions and ambivalences in their forms of queer world-making toward alternative futures.

7 Navigating Asian Pride from Sexual Citizenship and Governmentality Perspectives: Commentary by Mie Hiramoto

In this special collection of research making up this Element, examinations of Pride events in Asia are approached through the perspectives of language and sexuality. The origin of today's Pride events can be traced back to the Stonewall

Riots of 1969, which occurred in New York City, specifically at the Stonewall Inn, a gay bar in Greenwich Village (Armstrong and Crage, 2006; Duberman, 1993; Leap, 2020; Motschenbacher, 2020a). Throughout history LGBTQIA+ individuals have faced widespread discrimination, harassment, and violence from law enforcement and society at large, which set the backdrop for the events leading up to the Stonewall Riots. The Stonewall Inn, like many other establishments catering to the LGBTQIA+ community, was frequently raided by the police as part of a broader pattern of harassment and intimidation fuelled by institutionalized discrimination and societal prejudice against LGBTQIA+ individuals. These raids were often conducted under the guise of enforcing laws related to liquor licenses, operating hours, and indecent behavior, disproportionately targeting spaces known to be frequented by LGBTQIA+ people. On the night of June 28, 1969, patrons of the Stonewall Inn decided to resist the police raid, leading to several days of protests and demonstrations. This event came to be known as the Stonewall Riots and is often credited as the catalyst for the modern LGBTQIA+ rights movement in the US and around the world.

Following the Stonewall Riots, activists organized the first Christopher Street Liberation Day March, held on June 28, 1970, marking the first anniversary of the Stonewall uprising (Motschenbacher, 2020a, p. 65). This march is widely considered the precursor to today's Pride parades and events as it was a moment for LGBTQIA+ individuals to come together, assert their identities, demand equal rights and visibility, and celebrate their community (see Leap, 2020, for detailed discussion). Over time, Pride events have transformed into not just celebrations of LGBTQIA+ identity and culture but also forums for political activism, advocacy, and expressions of solidarity with marginalized communities, extending their influence beyond the borders of the United States to become a global phenomenon. The authors in this Element certainly prove this is true in the communities of different Asian cities they investigated. While Pride festivities vary in tone and focus around the world, they continue to honor the spirit of resistance and resilience born from the events of that fateful night at the Stonewall Inn. This is seen in all case studies featured in this volume; notably, a precursor to Pride in the Philippines is a public demonstration advocating for LGBTQIA+ rights known as Stonewall Manila in 1994 (see Go, 2022).

The contexts and case studies discussed in this volume highlight historicity, naturalization, and institutional marginalization of LGBTQIA+ people based on explicit power relationships in society. Genealogy, as employed by Foucault (1990), involves tracing the historical emergence and development of discourses, practices, and institutions to uncover the power relations and knowledge regimes that shape them. In his genealogical analyzes, Foucault examines how concepts such as governmentality and citizenship have evolved and how they are intertwined with broader systems of power and knowledge. He investigates the specific historical conditions and contingencies that have led to the emergence of particular modes of governance and forms of political subjectivity. From what we read, it is clear that individuals at the heart of Asian Pride have been placed in a specific stigmatized subject position (e.g., not ideal because of their nonconforming nature to essentialized gender ideologies).

Stigmatization of LGBTQIA+ individuals has existed in various forms throughout history across different cultures and regions, including in Asia. All the contributors explain that in places of their investigations, namely, Thailand, the Philippines, Taiwan, and Hong Kong, LGBTQIA+ individuals have faced societal stigmatization, discrimination, and legal challenges.

While the degree of stigmatization and discrimination may have varied across different periods and communities, historically, LGBTQIA+ people have often been marginalized and subjected to social ostracism in these regions due to conservative cultural, religious, and societal norms. By and large, Asia is known for its ideological alignment to gender and sexual essentialisms; thus, there have been systematic ways to discriminate against LGBTQIA+ individuals, such as through discriminatory laws, policies or societal attitudes. For example, laws denying same-sex marriage have been present in many Asian countries, in our case studies' context, except for Taiwan, leading to legal persecution and social marginalization of LGBTQIA+ individuals. By focusing on local Pride events and drawing on the LL methodology, each case study in this volume demonstrates how challenges and advocacy attempts can be unpacked from language and sexuality's viewpoints.

In the first case study, titled "Male Femininity, Citizenship, and Democracy in the Linguistic Landscape of a 'Pride' Protest in Bangkok," Pavadee Saisuwan reports on data collected from a protest event known as "Not a cutesy mob but a flamboyant one, sir, Mr. Government" which took place in July 2020, in the capital city of Thailand. She focuses on how *kathoey*ness – "Thai-specific male femininity" – was used in promoting LGBTQIA+ rights as well as democracy. In terms of LL, Saisuwan's analysis involves examining signage, public speeches, and other protest activities through the lens of Irvine and Gal's (2000) linguistic differentiation framework. The findings demonstrate the incorporation of various linguistic features of *kathoey*ness worked to bridge LGBTQIA+ and non-LGBTQIA+ individuals for a mutual goal of advocating for democracy against dictatorship. This idea of dictatorship limits the citizen's freedom at different levels and degrees, which includes an issue of institutional denial of LGBTQIA+ rights.

The next case study, Christian Go's "Spatializing the Intersections of Sexuality and Class in the Metro Manila Pride March" investigates the ways in which the 2023 MM Pride march highlights intersectional LGBTQIA+ activism in the capital city of the Philippines. Go tactfully showcases the LL data to examine how discursive and semiotic resources are utilized to advocate for the importance of passing national anti-discrimination legislation, referred to as the Sexual Orientation, Gender Identity, Gender Expression, or Sex Characteristics (SOGIESC) Bill. Go employs stance and stancetaking methodology through the lens of sexuality to underline evaluative, affective, and interpersonal aspects of protest signs and other semiotic resources found in the data. The findings suggest that discourses are adapted and negotiated surrounding sexual identity politics as well as socioeconomic and political issues in an intersectional manner. In summary, the combination of these discussions within the LGBTQIA+ community reflects the progression of MM Pride as a space for advocating across intersections and showing solidarity. Go's study adds to our comprehension of how a Pride event in an Asian setting provides insight into the role of intersectional dialogue in fostering different perspectives on Pride, as well as a collective effort to promote visibility, inclusivity, and societal transformation.

Li-Chi Chen showcases an LL analysis of Taiwan Pride from 2010 to 2020 in "Challenging Heteronormativity and Reifying *Tai*-ness: The Linguistic Landscape of Taiwan LGBT+ Pride." As explained by Chen, Taiwan's Pride started in 2003. In May 2019, Taiwan became the first country in Asia to legalize same-sex marriage, following a landmark ruling by the constitutional court in 2017 (see Ku, 2020). While the legislation allows same-sex couples to register their marriages and enjoy similar rights as heterosexual couples, Chen discusses how LGBTQIA+ community members still struggle against traditional Confucianism ideologies including gender-based essentialisms. Chen's decade-long data and analysis exhibits that Taiwanese Pride march participants have been challenging heteronormativity through homonormative practices such as the discursive and semiotic displays of noncisheteronormative desires. They foreground locally based identities in their protest messages along with their LGBTQIA+ identities such as their indigenousness or *tai*-ness – "Taiwanese localness."

The last case study in the examination of Asian Pride is Ben Rowlett's research titled "'Asia's World City' as Homotopia? Surveying Tensions in the Linguistic Landscape of the Hong Kong Gay Games." Unlike the preceding three case studies, Rowlett's study utilizes online discourse analytical methodology rather than on-site ethnographic research within Pride events. The focus shifts to analyzing the discursive portrayal of space through media representations, namely in local English news outlets, during the buildup to the Gay Games – an international LGBTQIA+ sporting and cultural event held in Asia (Hong Kong) for the first time in November 2023. Rowlett employs the concept of homotopia, drawn from sociolinguistic literature on sexuality and space, to investigate how socio-geopolitical discourses intersect with media representations of the event. The findings illuminate tensions surrounding issues of Pride, nationalism, security, and LGBTQIA+ rights, with Hong Kong media reflecting both global trends toward LGBTQIA+ inclusivity and resistance stemming from traditional conservatism, particularly regarding issues such as same-sex marriage.

Coming back to Foucault, he argued that institutional power led to a significant change in the way sexuality was understood, shifting the focus from mere sexual desire to the concept of sexual identity. This shift was marked by the introduction of terms such as "heterosexual" and "homosexual" within medical discourse. Previously, sexuality had been primarily viewed in terms of desire, but the emergence of these terms initiated a new understanding centered on distinct sexual personality types, or "sexual identities," which continue to hold sway in contemporary discourse. Foucault also examined how power operates within societies and how individuals are governed and regulated by various institutions and discourses. Governmentality refers to the techniques and strategies through which populations are governed. Foucault (1977) argues that modern forms of power operate through not only direct coercion but also more subtle mechanisms of control, such as surveillance, normalization (naturalization), and the shaping of subjectivities. Governmentality encompasses a broad range of practices, including political governance, economic management, social welfare policies, and cultural norms. Foucault's analysis of governmentality highlights how power is dispersed and exercised through networks of institutions, technologies, and discourses. He emphasizes the role of knowledge and expertise in governing populations, as well as how individuals internalize and comply with governing norms and regulations.

Relatedly, with citizenship, Foucault (2008) problematizes traditional understandings of citizenship as a status granted by the state. He argues that citizenship is not simply a legal category but also a site of power relations and subjectivation. Foucault explores how citizenship is shaped by regimes of knowledge, practices of inclusion and exclusion, and modes of subjectification. His work on governmentality and citizenship encourages critical reflection on the complexities of power and governance in modern societies, and I must say that all case studies in this Element do an excellent job of demonstrating critical reflections found in their data and context. By employing a genealogical approach, Foucault seeks to disrupt linear narratives of progress and to reveal the contingent and contested nature of social and political phenomena. Emphasizing local historicity Saisuwan, Go, Chen, and Rowlett highlight how power operates through discontinuities, ruptures, and struggles, rather than through smooth and coherent processes of development with their studies and point out the way in which systematized naturalization and institutional marginalization of LGBTQIA+ people have been taking place.

In light of the nuanced explorations within this Element, it becomes evident that the intersections of governmentality and sexual citizenship across diverse Asian contexts align closely with Foucault's genealogical approach. By highlighting the intricate dynamics of power and knowledge over time, these discussions underscore the importance of understanding the historical contexts in which systems of governance and identity formation operate today. Through this lens, the narratives of/about sexual minorities in Asia not only illuminate the complexities of their lived experiences but also offer valuable insights into broader sociopolitical landscapes. The theoretical depth and analytical rigor demonstrated throughout this volume significantly enhance our understanding of the complex dynamics shaping the experiences and struggles of sexual minorities in Asia, making it a valuable contribution to scholarship in the broad field of language, gender, and sexuality.

References

Akkaravisitpol, W. (2021). Kan suesan phang kha wiwat kap prakotkan flash mob yaowachon thai [Disruptive communication and flash mob of Thai youth]. *Warasan Nithet Sat Parithat* [Journal of Communication Arts Review], 25(1), 60–69.

Alfredsson, J., and Augustsson, L. (2017). The next wave of the suit-era: A forecasting model of the men's suit. Unpublished master's thesis, University of Borås.

Altman, D. (1997). Global gaze/global gays. *GLQ: A Journal of Lesbian and Gay Studies*, 3(4), 417–436.

Ammaturo, F. R. (2016). Spaces of pride: A visual ethnography of gay pride parades in Italy and the United Kingdom. *Social Movement Studies*, 15(1), 19–40. https://doi.org/10.1080/14742837.2015.1060156

Armstrong, E. A., and Crage, S. M. (2006). Movements and memory: The making of the Stonewall myth. *American Sociological Review*, 71(5), 724–751. https://doi.org/10.1177/000312240607100502

Bacchetta, P., and Haritaworn, J. (2011). There are many transatlantics: Homonationalism, homotransnationalism and feminist-queer-trans of colour theories and practices. In M. Evans, ed., *Transatlantic Conversations: Feminism as Travelling Theory*. Farnham: Ashgate, pp. 127–143.

Baudinette, T. (2017). The spatialisation of desire in a Japanese gay district through signage. *ACME: An International Journal for Critical Geographies*, 16(3), 500–527.

Baudinette, T. (2018). Cosmopolitan English, traditional Japanese: Reading language desire into the signage of Tokyo's gay district. *Linguistic Landscape*, 4(3), 238–256. https://doi.org/10.1075/ll.18004.bau

Ben-Rafael, E. (2009). A sociological approach to the study of linguistic landscapes. In E. Shohamy and D. Gorter, eds., *Linguistic Landscape: Expanding the Scenery*. New York: Routledge, pp. 40–54.

Bergling, T. (2001). *Sissyphobia: Gay Men and Effeminate Behavior*. New York: Harrington Park Press.

Blommaert, J. (2019). From groups to actions and back in online–offline sociolinguistics. *Multilingua*, 38(4), 485–493. https://doi.org/10.1515/multi-2018-0114

Bogetić, K. (2020). Co-opting the neoliberal manhood ideal: Masculinity, normativity, and recursive normalisation in Serbian gay men's digital dating profiles. *Language in Society*, 50(1), 93–123. https://doi.org/10.1017/S0047404520000639

Borba, R., and Hiramoto, M. (2024). From top to bottom (and back!): Gender and sexuality in linguistic landscapes. In R. Blackwood, S. Tufi, and W. Amos, eds., *The Bloomsbury Handbook of Linguistic Landscapes*. London: Bloomsbury, pp. 218–234.

Bucholtz, M., and Hall, K. (2010). Locating identity in language. In C. Llamas and D. Watt, eds., *Language and Identities*. Edinburgh: Edinburgh University Press, pp. 18–28.

Canakis, C., and Kersten-Pejanić, R. (2016). Spray-canned discourses: Reimagining gender, sexuality, and citizenship through linguistic landscapes in the Balkans. In S. Goll, M. Mlinaric, and J. Gold, eds., *Minorities Under Attack: Othering and Right-Wing Extremism in Southeast European Societies*. Wiesbaden: Harrassowitz, pp. 129–160.

Chen, K.-H. (2010). *Asia as Method: Toward Deimperialization*. Durham, NC: Duke University Press.

Chen, L.-C. (2017). *Taiwanese and Polish Humor: A Socio-Pragmatic Analysis*. Newcastle upon Tyne: Cambridge Scholars Publishing.

Chen, L.-C. (2022). Humour and teasing in gay Taiwanese men's mediatised interaction on an LGBTQ-oriented YouTube entertainment variety show. *Gender and Language*, 16(4), 408–434. https://doi.org/10.1558/genl.18746

Chen, L.-C. (2023). "Smash this sissy boy's mouth, Cuiguo!": Framing and humor in gay Taiwanese YouTubers' self-disclosures about being bullied. *Discourse & Communication*, 17(2), 135–154. https://doi.org/10.1177/17504813221132978

Chen-Dedman, A. (2023). *Tongzhi* sovereignty: Taiwan's LGBT rights movement and the misplaced critique of homonationalism. *International Journal of Taiwan Studies*, 6(2), 261–290. https://doi.org/10.1163/24688800-20221267

Chiang, H., and Wong, A. K. (2016). Queering the transnational turn: Regionalism and queer Asias. *Gender, Place & Culture*, 23(11), 1643–1656.

Chua, L. J. (2012). Pragmatic resistance, law, and social movements in authoritarian states: The case of gay collective action in Singapore. *Law & Society Review*, 46(4), 713–748.

Chuipracha, D. (2020). How to neramit 'mob mai mungming tae tungting kha khun ratthaban' mob thi creative lae pang pu ri ye thisut haeng yuk samai [How to create "Not a cutesy mob but a flamboyant one, sir, Mr. Government": The most creative and impressive protest of the era], *a day*, November 2. https://adaymagazine.com/how-to-create-mob-mai-mungming/

Comer, J. (2022). *Discourses of Global Queer Mobility and the Mediatization of Equality*. New York: Routledge.

Conway, D. (2023). The politics of truth at LGBTQ+ Pride: Contesting corporate Pride and revealing marginalized lives at Hong Kong Migrants Pride. *International Feminist Journal of Politics*, 25(4), 734–756.

Cruz, B. M. D. (2023). House legislators file magna carta for BPO workers bill. *BusinessWorld*, May 18. www.bworldonline.com/economy/2023/05/18/523774/house-legislators-file-magna-carta-for-bpo-workers-bill/

Davidson, J. (2013). Sporting homonationalisms: Sexual exceptionalism, queer privilege, and the 21st century international lesbian and gay sport movement. *Sociology of Sport Journal*, 30(1), 57–82. https://doi.org/10.1123/ssj.30.1.57

Duangwises, N., and Jackson, P. A. (2021). Effeminacy and masculinity in Thai gay culture: Language, contextuality and the enactment of gender plurality. *Asia Social Issues*, 14(5), 1–23.

Du Bois, J. W. (2007). The stance triangle. In R. Englebretson, ed., *Stancetaking in Discourse: Subjectivity, Evaluation, Interaction*. Amsterdam: John Benjamins, pp. 139–182.

Duberman, M. B. (1993). *Stonewall*. New York: Dutton.

Duggan, L. (2002). The new homonormativity: The sexual politics of neoliberalism. In R. Castronovo and D. D. Nelson, eds., *Materializing Democracy: Toward a Revitalized Cultural Politics*. Durham, NC: Duke University Press, pp. 175–194.

Eguchi, S. (2009). Negotiating hegemonic masculinity: The rhetorical strategy of "straight-acting" among gay men. *Journal of Intercultural Communication Research*, 38(3), 193–209. https://doi.org/10.1080/17475759.2009.508892

Einwohner, R. L., Kelly-Thompson, K., Sinclair-Chapman, V., Tormos-Aponte, F., Weldon, S. L., Wright, J. M., and Wu, C. (2021). Active solidarity: Intersectional solidarity in action. *Social Politics: International Studies in Gender, State & Society*, 28(3), 704–729. https://doi.org/10.1093/sp/jxz052

Engel, S. M. (2001). *The Unfinished Revolution: Social Movement Theory and the Gay and Lesbian Movement*. New York: Cambridge University Press.

Evangelista, J. A. G. (2017). Mula sa kinaroroonang ideolohiya: Kontrobersya sa tungkol sa "unang" Pride March sa Pilipinas. *Saliksik*, 6(2), 256–296.

Faulkner, L. (2021). Hong Kong supports Gay Games and LGBT rights, but Legco does not reflect that. *South China Morning Post*, June 14. www.scmp.com/comment/letters/article/3136940/hong-kong-supports-gay-games-and-lgbt-rights-legco-does-not-reflect

Foucault, M. (1977). *Discipline and Punish: The Birth of the Prison*. London: Vintage Books.

Foucault, M. (1986). Of other spaces: Utopias and heterotopias. Trans. J. Miskowiec. *Diacritics 16*, 22–27.

Foucault, M. (1990). *The History of Sexuality: An Introduction*. Vol. 1. Harmondsworth: Penguin.

Foucault, M. (2001). Truth and power. In James D. Faubion and Robert Hurley, eds., *Power: The Essential Works of Foucault, 1954–1984, Vol. 3*. New York: New Press, pp. 111–133.

Foucault, M. (2008). *The Birth of Biopolitics*. Trans. G. Burchell. London: Palgrave Macmillan.

Gay Games 11 Hong Kong 2023. (2020). Get ready and get involved now at Gay Games 11 Hong Kong 11–19 November 2022! Online video clip. November 10. www.youtube.com/watch?v=otJx5CW_P-o

Go, C. (2022). Queerly spaced: Signs, affect and stancetaking in the linguistic landscape of the Metro Manila Pride March. PhD diss., National University of Singapore. https://scholarbank.nus.edu.sg/handle/10635/216514

Go, C. (2024). Landscaping gender, sexuality, and hope in the 2022 Philippine presidential elections. *Linguistic Landscape*, ahead of print, August 5, 2024. https://doi.org/10.1075/ll.24006.go

Gopinath, G. (2007). Queer region: Locating lesbians in Sancharram. In G. E. Haggerty and M. Mcgarry, eds., *A Companion to Lesbian, Gay, Bisexual, Transgender, and Queer Studies*. Malden, MA: Blackwell, pp. 341–354.

Gorter, D. (2019). Methods and techniques for linguistic landscape research: About definitions, core issues and technological innovations. In M. Pütz and M. Mundt, eds., *Expanding the Linguistic Landscape: Linguistic Diversity, Multimodality and the Use of Space as a Semiotic Resource*. Bristol: Multilingual Matters, pp. 38–57.

Guy, P. (2017). The Gay Games is Hong Kong's moment to show the city's inclusivity. Are we ready? *South China Morning Post*, November 5. www.scmp.com/business/article/2118441/gay-games-hong-kongs-moment-show-our-citys-inclusivity-are-we-ready

Haarmann, H. (1989). *Symbolic Values of Foreign Language Use: From the Japanese Case to a General Sociolinguistic Perspecive*. Berlin: Mouton de Gruyter.

Hajndrych, E., and Wu, T.-H. (2022). Rìzhì shíqí Táiwān nǚxìng de chǔjìng: Yǐ *Táiwān Xīnmínbào* de gēyáo wéi zhōngxīn [Women's circumstances in Japan-ruled Taiwan: Analyzing folk songs in *Taiwan New People Newspaper*]. In Sekiguchi Global Research Association, ed., *Ajia no Mirai e: Watashi no Teian, Vol. 6A* [*Toward the Future of Asia: My Proposal, Vol. 6A*]. Tokyo: The Japan Times, pp. 135–140.

Hall, K. (2019). Middle class timelines: Ethnic humor and sexual modernity in Delhi. *Language in Society*, 48(4), 491–517. https://doi.org/10.1017/S0047404519000435

Hawae, P. (2020). 'Mob mai mungming tae tungting kha khun ratthaban' chutyuen klum khon laklai thang phet nai wethi kanmueang ["Not a cutesy mob but a flamboyant one, sir, Mr. Government": The stance of LGBTQIA+ on the political stage], *The Standard*, 26 July. https://thestandard.co/lgbtq-stance-on-politics/

Hiramoto, M. (2017). Powerfully queered: Representations of castrated male characters in Chinese martial arts films. *Gender and Language*, 11(4), 529–551. https://doi.org/10.1558/genl.31592

Ho, M.-S. (2019). Taiwan's road to marriage equality: Politics of legalizing same-sex marriage. *China Quarterly*, 238, 482–503. https://doi.org/10.1017/S0305741018001765

Ho, M.-S., and Blackwood, E. (2022). Queer Asias: Genders and sexualities across borders and boundaries. *Sexualities*, 27(1–2), 68–76.

Hodges, A. (2015). Intertextuality in discourse. In D. Tannen, H. E. Hamilton, and D. Schiffrin, eds., *The Handbook of Discourse Analysis*. Malden, MA: Wiley Blackwell, pp. 42–60. https://doi.org/10.1002/9781118584194.ch2

Holliday, R. (2001). Fashioning the queer self. In J. Entwistle and E. Wilson, eds., *Body Dressing*. Oxford: Berg, pp. 215–232.

Holmes, A. (2021). Marching with Pride? Debates on uniformed police participation in Vancouver's LGBTQ Pride parade. *Journal of Homosexuality*, 68(8), 1320–1352. https://doi.org/10.1080/00918369.2019.1696107

Hunt, S., and Holmes, C. (2015). Everyday decolonization: Living a decolonizing queer politics. *Journal of Lesbian Studies*, 19(2), 154–172.

Interpride. (2020). 2020 Annual Report. www.interpride.org/wp-content/uploads/2022/08/IP_2020_Annual-Report.pdf

Intorn, T. (2021). Sue sangkhom online kap kan prathuang rupbaep mai: Korani khabuankan khlueanwai thang kanmueang thai 2563 [Social media and new form of protest: A case of the Thailand's 2020 political movements]. *Warasan Ratthasat Phichan* [Political Science Critique], 8(16), 50–74.

Irvine, J. T., and Gal, S. (2000). Language ideology and linguistic differentiation. In P. V. Kroskrity, ed., *Regimes of Language: Ideologies, Polities, and Identities*. Santa Fe: School of American Research Press, pp. 35–84.

Isin, E. (2017). Performative citizenship. In A. Shachar, R. Bauböck, I. Bloemraad, and M. Vink, eds., *The Oxford Handbook of Citizenship*. Oxford: Oxford University Press, pp. 500–523.

Jackson, P. A. (1997). *Kathoey* >< gay >< man: The historical emergence of gay male identity in Thailand. In L. Manderson and M. Jolly, eds., *Sites of Desire,*

Economies of Pleasure: Sexualities in Asia and the Pacific. Chicago: University of Chicago Press, pp. 166–190.

Jackson, P. A. (2004). *Gay* adaptation, *tom-dee* resistance, and *kathoey* indifference: Thailand's gender/sex minorities and the episodic allure of queer English. In W. L. Leap and T. Boellstorff, eds., *Speaking in Queer Tongues: Globalization and Gay Languages*. Urbana: University of Illinois Press, pp. 202–230.

Jaffe, A. (2009). *Stance: Sociolinguistic Perspectives*. Oxford: Oxford University Press.

Jaworski, A., and Thurlow, C. (2010). Introducing semiotic landscapes. In A. Jaworski and C. Thurlow, eds., *Semiotic Landscapes: Language, Image, Space*. London: Continuum, pp. 1–40.

Jiang. S. (2020). "End of the rainbow": Shanghai Pride shuts down amid shrinking space for China's LGBTQ community. *CNN*, August 16. https://edition.cnn.com/2020/08/14/asia/shanghai-pride-shutdown-intl-hnk/index.html

Johnstone, B. (2010). Indexing the local. In N. Coupland, ed., *Handbook of Language and Globalization*. Oxford: Oxford University Press, pp. 386–405.

Kiesling, S. F. (2022). Stance and stancetaking. *Annual Review of Linguistics*, 8, 409–426. https://doi.org/10.1146/annurev-linguistics-031120-121256

Kitagawa, C., and Lehrer, A. (1990). Impersonal uses of personal pronouns. *Journal of Pragmatics*, 14(5), 739–759. https://doi.org/10.1016/0378-2166(90)90004-W

Kong, T. S. K. (2019) Transnational queer sociological analysis of sexual identity and civic–political activism in Hong Kong, Taiwan and Mainland China. *British Journal of Sociology*, 70(5), 1904–1925. https://doi.org/10.1111/1468-4446.12697

Kong, T. S. K. (2023). *Sexuality and the Rise of China: The Post-1990s Gay Generation in Hong Kong, Taiwan, and Mainland China*. Durham, NC: Duke University Press.

Kraijariyawet, W. (2021). Botbat khong khabuankan khlueanwai thang sangkhom "klum nakrian leo' nai kan phlakdan nayobai dan kansueksa [The roles of the movement "Bad Student Group" in pushing education policy]. Master's thesis, Srinakharinwirot University. http://ir-ithesis.swu.ac.th/dspace/handle/123456789/1722

Ku, E. K. (2020). "Waiting for my red envelope": Discourses of sameness in the linguistic landscape of a marriage equality demonstration in Taiwan. *Critical Discourse Studies*, 17(2), 156–174. https://doi.org/10.1080/17405904.2019.1656655

Kuo, S.-H. (2002). From solidarity to antagonism: The use of the second-person singular pronoun in Chinese political discourse. *Text & Talk: An Interdisciplinary Journal of Language, Discourse & Communication Studies*, 22(1), 29–55. https://doi.org/10.1515/text.2002.004

Lai, F. Y. (2024). Migrant workers and LGBT activism: A comparative study of Filipino and Indonesian domestic workers in Hong Kong. *Sexualities*, 27(1–2), 113–135.

Lau, C., and Cheng, L. (2021). Hong Kong leader Carrie Lam says city will support Gay Games, and calls lawmaker's hate-filled outburst 'unnecessarily divisive'. *South China Morning Post*, June 15. www.scmp.com/news/hong-kong/politics/article/3137333/hong-kong-leader-carrie-lam-says-city-will-support-gay

Lau, H., Loper, K., and Suen, Y. T. (2023). Support in Hong Kong for same-sex couples' rights grew over ten years (2013–2023): 60 percent now support same-sex marriage. Briefing Report, *Centre for Comparative and Public Law at the Faculty of Law, The University of Hong Kong Sexualities Research Programme, The Chinese University of Hong Kong Human Rights Law Program, and University of North Carolina School of Law*.

Lazar, M. M. (2017). Homonationalist discourse as a politics of pragmatic resistance in Singapore's Pink Dot movement: Towards a southern praxis. *Journal of Sociolinguistics*, 21(3), 420–441. https://doi.org/10.1111/josl.12239

Lazar, M. M. (2021). Gender and sexuality in discourse. In J. Angouri and J. Baxter, eds., *The Routledge Handbook of Language, Gender, and Sexuality*. London: Routledge, pp. 481–493.

Leap, W. L. (2020). *Language Before Stonewall: Language, Sexuality, History*. Basingstoke: Palgrave Macmillan.

Lee, D. (2017). Calls for Hong Kong to better protect LGBT rights as city wins bid to host 2022 Gay Games. South China Morning Post, October 31. www.scmp.com/news/hong-kong/community/article/2117697/hong-kong-wins-bid-host-2022-gay-olympics

Lee, P.-H. (2017). Queer activism in Taiwan: An emergent rainbow coalition from the assemblage perspective. *Sociological Review*, 65(4), 682–698. https://doi.org/10.1177/0038026116681441

Lertchoosakul, K. (2021). The white ribbon movement: High school students in the 2020 Thai youth protests. *Critical Asian Studies*, 53(2), 206–218. https://doi.org/10.1080/14672715.2021.1883452

Levon, E. (2020). Language, (in)security, and sexuality. *Journal of Sociolinguistics*, 24(1), 111–118.

Li, P.-W., and Lu, C.-R. (2020). Articulating sexuality, desire, and identity: A keyword analysis of heteronormativity in Taiwanese gay and lesbian dating websites. *Sexuality & Culture*, 24(5), 1499–1521. https://doi.org/10.1007/s12119-020-09709-5

Liao, P.-R. (2020). "Only filial piety can produce heirs, not homosexuals!": An exploration of the glocalised rhetoric of the pro-family movement in Taiwan. *Culture and Religion: An Interdisciplinary Journal*. 21(2), 139–156. https://doi.org/10.1080/14755610.2021.1906726

Lou, J. J. (2017). Spaces of consumption and senses of place: A geosemiotic analysis of three markets in Hong Kong. *Social Semiotics*, 27(4), 513–531. https://doi.org/10.1080/10350330.2017.1334403

Luther, J. D., and Loh, J. U. (2019) *"Queer" Asia: Decolonizing and Reimagining Sexuality and Gender*. London: Zed Books.

Maly, I., and Blommaert, J. (2019). Digital ethnographic linguistic landscape analysis (ELLA 2.0). *Tilburg Papers in Culture Studies*, 233, 1–26.

Marino, F. (2023). # Twospirit: Identity construction through stance-taking on TikTok. *Discourse, Context & Media*, 54, 100711. https://doi.org/10.1016/j.dcm.2023.100711.

Markwell, K., and Waitt, G (2009). Festivals, space and sexuality: Gay pride in Australia. *Tourism Geographies*, 11(2), 143–168. https://doi.org/10.1080/14616680902827092

Milani, T. M. (2014). Sexed signs: Queering the scenery. *International Journal of the Sociology of Language*, 228, 201–205. https://doi.org/10.1515/ijsl-2014-0011

Milani, T. M. (2015). Sexual cityzenship: Discourses, spaces and bodies at Joburg Pride 2012. *Journal of Language and Politics*, 14(3), 431–454. https://doi.org/10.1075/jlp.14.3.06mil

Milani, T. M., and Kapa, K (2015). Ready-to-wear sexual politics: The semiotics of visibility on Wits Pride t-shirts. *Stellenbosch Papers in Linguistics Plus*, 46, 79–103.

Milani, T. M., and Lazar, M. M. (2017). Seeing from the South: Discourse, gender and sexuality from southern perspectives. *Journal of Sociolinguistics*, 21(3), 307–319. https://doi.org/10.1111/josl.12241

Milani, T. M., and Levon, E. (2016). Sexing diversity: Linguistic landscapes of homonationalism. *Language & Communication*, 51, 69–86. https://doi.org/10.1016/j.langcom.2016.07.002

Milani, T. M., and Levon, E. (2019). Israel as Homotopia: Language, space and vicious belonging. *Language in Society*, 48(4), 607–628. https://doi.org/10.1017/S0047404519000356

Milani, T. M., and Levon, E. (2024). Theorizing checkpoints of desire: Multilingualism, sexuality and (in)security in Israel-Palestine. *International Journal of Bilingual Education and Bilingualism*, 27(5), 702–714. https://doi.org/10.1080/13670050.2024.2306390

Milani, T. M., Levon, E., Gafter, R. J., and Or, I. G. (2018). Tel Aviv as a space of affirmation versus transformation: Language, citizenship, and the politics of sexuality in Israel. *Linguistic Landscape*, 4(3), 278–297. https://doi.org/10.1075/ll.18006.mil

Moeller, K. (2003). Chinese women unbound: An analysis of women's emancipation in China. *Inquiry: The University of Arkansas Undergraduate Research Journal*, 4(1), 69–77.

Mok, D. (2021). Hong Kong Gay Games needs more support, lawmaker Regina Ip says as event struggles to find venues. *South China Morning Post*, June 9. www.scmp.com/news/hong-kong/society/article/3136702/hong-kong-gay-games-needs-more-support-lawmaker-regina-ip

Mono News. (2020). [Twitter] July 25. https://twitter.com/mthai/status/1287052206340857857?s=20

Moser, D. (1997). Covert sexism in Mandarin Chinese. *Sino-Platonic Papers*, 74, 1–23.

Motschenbacher, H. (2020a). Language use before and after Stonewall: A corpus-based study of gay men's pre-Stonewall narratives. *Discourse Studies*, 22(1), 64–86. https://doi.org/10.1177/1461445619887541

Motschenbacher, H. (2020b). Walking on Wilton Drive: A linguistic landscape analysis of a homonormative space. *Language & Communication*, 72, 25-43. https://doi.org/10.1016/j.langcom.2020.02.002

Motschenbacher, H. (2023). Affective regimes on Wilton Drive: A multimodal analysis. *Social Semiotics*, 33(1), 168–187. https://doi.org/10.1080/10350330.2020.1788823

Mowlabocus, S. (2023). Fucking with homonormativity: The ambiguous politics of chemsex. *Sexualities*, 26(5–6), 585–603. https://doi.org/10.1177/1363460721999267

Ng, E, and Li, X. (2022). Brand nohomonationalism: *Guofeng* ('national style') framings of Boys' Love television series in China. *Asian Studies Review*, 47(3), 613–630. https://doi.org/10.1080/10357823.2022.2142933

Ng, K-c. (2021). Hong Kong Gay Games 'a wolf in sheep's clothing' and threat to national security, lawmakers warn. *South China Morning Post*, August 25. www.scmp.com/news/hong-kong/society/article/3146387/hong-kong-gay-games-wolf-sheeps-clothing-and-threat-national

Ning, Y.-B. (2018). Fěnshì yǔ tóngxìngliàn mínzú zhǔyì zhīhòu: Yīyízhìyí xià de zhīshì shēngchǎn [Pinkwashing, homonationalism and the politics of colored people knowledge-production]. *Táiwān Shèhuì Yánjiù Jìkān* [Taiwan: A Radical Quarterly in Social Studies], 111, 231–248.

Ong, F., Lewis, C., and Vorobjovas-Pinta, O. (2021). Questioning the inclusivity of events: The queer perspective. *Journal of Sustainable Tourism*, 29(11–12), 2044–2061. https://doi.org/10.1080/09669582.2020.1860072

Outright International. (2021). Pride around the world https://outrightinternational.org/sites/default/files/2023-03/Outright_PrideAroundTheWorld2021.pdf

Outright International. (2022). Visible: Pride around the world. https://outright-international.org/sites/default/files/2023-04/Outright_PrideRevised2022English.pdf

Pak, V. (2023). Lighting, signing, showing: The circulability of Pink Dot's counterpublic discourse in Singapore. *Journal of Sociolinguistics*, 27(1), 24–41. https://doi.org/10.1111/josl.12568

Pak, V., and Hiramoto, M. (2021). For family, for friends, for (true) love: Negotiating discourses of love within the LGBTQ community in Singapore. *Journal of Language and Sexuality*, 10(2), 105–128. https://doi.org/10.1075/jls.20009.hir

Paradela, T. (2019). Tracing the origins of the Metro Manila Pride March. *SPOT.ph*, June 29. www.spot.ph/newsfeatures/the-latest-news-features/78298/history-of-pride-march-in-the-philippines-a4410-20190629-lfrm

Pelclová, J. (2023). Stance-taking as an identity construction in advertising targeted at mothers: A comparative analysis. *Studies About Languages*, 42, 93–104. https://doi.org/10.5755/j01.sal.1.42.33341

Pennycook, A. (2017). Translanguaging and semiotic assemblages. *International Journal of Multilingualism*, 14(3), 269–282. https://doi.org/10.1080/14790718.2017.1315810

Phillips, R (2013). "We aren't really that different": Globe-hopping discourse and queer rights in Singapore. *Journal of Language and Sexuality*, 2(1), 122–144. https://doi.org/10.1075/jls.2.1.05phi

Plummer, K. (1992). *Modern Homosexualities*. London: Routledge.

Puar, J. K. (2007). *Terrorist Assemblages: Homonationalism in Queer Times*. Durham, NC: Duke University Press.

Purdie-Vaughns, V., and Eibach, R. P. (2008). Intersectional invisibility: The distinctive advantages and disadvantages of multiple subordinate-group identities. *Sex Roles: A Journal of Research*, 59(5–6), 377–391. https://doi.org/10.1007/s11199-008-9424-4

Rampton, B., and Charalambous, C. (2020). Sociolinguistics and everyday (in) securitization. *Journal of Sociolinguistics*, 24(1), 75–88.

Raptor eng cha. (2020). [Twitter] July 24. https://twitter.com/RTsiraphop/status/1286496530879221760?s=20

Richardson, D. (1998). Sexuality and citizenship. *Sociology*, 32(1), 83–100. www.jstor.org/stable/42855899

Richardson, D. (2000). Constructing sexual citizenship: Theorizing sexual rights. *Critical Social Policy*, 20(1), 105–135. https://doi.org/10.1177/026101830002000105

Rinna pa Pepsi thung. (2020). [Twitter] July 25. https://twitter.com/rinna12731/status/1287019123294081027?s=20

Roth, S. (2021). Intersectionality and coalitions in social movement research: A survey and outlook. *Sociology Compass*, 15(7), e12885. https://doi.org/10.1111/soc4.12885

Rowlett, B. J. L., and Go, C. (2021). Tracing trans-regional discursive flows in Pink Dot Hong Kong promotional videos: (Homo)normativities and nationalism, activism and ambivalence. *Journal of Language and Sexuality*, 10(2), 158–180. https://doi.org/10.1075/jls.20007.row

Rowlett, B. J. L., and Go, C. (2024). "The amazingly fabulous tuk tuk race": Mobility and carnival praxis in the semiotic landscape of Phnom Penh Pride. *Social Semiotics* 24(3), 430–448.

Ruan, C., and Du, J.-X. (2009). "Bàoqiàn," "dàoqiàn" hé "duìbùqǐ" biànxī [A comparative study of "baoqian," "daoqian" and "duibuqi"]. *Tángshān Xuéyuàn Xuébào* [Journal of Tangshan College], 22(2), 54–56.

Saisuwan, P. (2016). *Kathoey* and the linguistic construction of gender identity in Thailand. In E. Levon and R. B. Mendes, eds., *Language, Sexuality, and Power: Studies in Intersectional Sociolinguistics*. Oxford: Oxford University Press, pp. 189–214.

Salonga, A. O. (2015). Performing gayness and English in an offshore call center industry. In R. Tupas, ed., *Unequal Englishes: The Politics of Englishes Today*. London: Palgrave Macmillan, pp. 130–142.

Sánchez, F. J., and Vilain, E. (2012). "Straight-acting gays": The relationship between masculine consciousness, anti-effeminacy, and negative gay identity. *Archives of Sexual Behavior: The Official Publication of the International Academy of Sex Research*, 41, 111–119. https://doi.org/10.1007/s10508-012-9912-z

Santino, J. (2011). The carnivalesque and the ritualesque. *Journal of American Folklore*, 124(491), 61–73. https://doi.org/10.5406/jamerfolk.124.491.0061

Santos, J. A. L., and Saisuwan, P. (2023). "Dream Boy" and "Hotmale": The semiotic landscape of queer space in Bangkok. *Manusya: Journal of Humanities*, 26(1), 1–22. https://doi.org/10.1163/26659077-25010025

Sarce, J. P. (2023). From aura to awra: Toward a tropical queer decolonial performativity in the Philippines. *eTropic: Electronic Journal of Studies in the Tropics*, 22(1), 29–52. http://dx.doi.org/10.25120/etropic.22.1.2023.3966

SCMP Editorial (2021). Reject bigotry and get behind Hong Kong's Gay Games. *South China Morning Post*, June 22. www.scmp.com/comment/opinion/article/3138229/reject-bigotry-and-get-behind-hong-kongs-gay-games

Seals, C. A. (2017). Analyzing the linguistic landscape of mass-scale events. *Linguistic Landscape*, 3(3), 267–285.

Shirinian, T., and Channell-Justice, E. (2020). Introduction: Of constatives, performatives, and disidentifications: Decolonizing queer critique in post-socialist times. In E. Channell-Justice (ed.), *Decolonizing Queer Experience: LGBT+ Narratives from Eastern Europe and Eurasia*. Washington, DC: Lexington Books, pp. 1–14.

Shohamy, E., and Ben-Rafael, E. (2015). Introduction: Linguistic landscape. A new journal *Linguistic Landscape*, 1(1/2), 1–5. https://doi org/10.1075/ll.1.1-2.001int

Sinpeng, A. (2021). Hashtag activism: Social media and the #FreeYouth protests in Thailand. *Critical Asian Studies*, 53(2), 192–205. https://doi.org/10.1080/14672715.2021.1882866

Sinpongsaporn, W. (2020). Bot wikhro kanmueang lang 15 tulakhom 63 "sing thi rao rianru chak churnnum klangmueang" [Analysis of the post-October 15, 2020 political landscape: "Lessons learned from the downtown protests"], *workpointTODAY*, October 16. https://workpointtoday.com/opinion/

Skidmore, P. L. (1999). Dress to impress: Employer regulation of gay and lesbian appearance. *Social and Legal Studies*, 8(4), 509–529. https://doi.org/10.1177/a010360

Su, H.-Y. (2008). What does it mean to be a girl with *qizhi*?: Refinement, gender and language ideologies in contemporary Taiwan. *Journal of Sociolinguistics*, 12(3), 334–358. https://doi.org/10.1111/j.1467-9841.2008.00370.x

Su, H.-Y. (2011). The meaning contestation of *tai*: Language ideologies and the global–local ambivalence. *Concentric: Studies in Linguistics*, 37(2), 283–308.

Su, H.-Y. (2018). Contested words, gender norms and language ideologies: The gendered meaning of *tai*. *Gender and Language*, 12(1), 27–60. https://doi.org/10.1558/genl.28954

Su, H.-Y. (2023). Mothers as stancetakers: Intertextuality in same-sex marriage debates in Taiwan. *Discourse & Society*, 34(2), 192–212. https://doi.org/10.1177/09579265221117048

Symons, C. (2010). *The Gay Games*. London: Routledge.

Thanapornsangsuth, S., and Anamwathana, P. (2022). Youth participation during Thailand's 2020–2021 political turmoil. *Asia Pacific Journal of Education*, 1–15. https://doi.org/10.1080/02188791 2022.2037513

Valmores-Salinas, R. (2020). More than just a murder. *Philstar Global*, September 11. www.philstar.com/lifestyle/young-star/2020/09/11/2041453/more-just-murder

Waitt, G. R. (2006). Boundaries of desire: Becoming sexual through the spaces of Sydney's 2002 Gay Games. *Annals of the Association of American Geographers*, 96(4), 773–787. https://doi.org/10.1111/j.1467-8306.2006.00811.x

Wang, C. (2021). Hong Kong's Gay Games pushed to 2023 due to city's strict Covid-19 quarantine rules. *South China Morning Post*, September 15. www.scmp.com/news/hong-kong/politics/article/3148801/hong-kongs-gay-games-pushed-2023-due-strict-covid-19

Wang, A., and Taylor, J. (2021). Taiwan won't attend Hong Kong's Gay Games fearing security law. *Hong Kong Free Press*, August 6. https://hongkongfp.com/2021/08/06/taiwan-wont-attend-hong-kongs-gay-games-fearing-security-law/

Warner, M. (1991). Introduction: Fear of a queer planet. *Social Text*, 29, 3-17.

Webb, A. (2022). *Chasing Freedom: The Philippines' Long Journey to Democratic Ambivalence*. Liverpool: Liverpool University Press.

Wilson, J. (1990). *Politically Speaking: The Pragmatic Analysis of Political Language*. Oxford: Basil Blackwell.

Wong, B. W. S. (2021) Why Gay Games give Hong Kong a chance to bolster its fading reputation. *South China Morning Post*, June 17. www.scmp.com/comment/opinion/article/3137381/why-gay-games-give-hong-kong-chance-bolster-its-fading-reputation

Wu, A. (2021) Hong Kong Gay Games: Prejudice and hatred in Legco fall foul of Beijing's desire for social harmony. *South China Morning Post*, June 14. www.scmp.com/comment/opinion/article/3136986/hong-kong-gay-games-prejudice-and-hatred-legco-fall-foul-beijings

Yu, Y., and Nartey, M. (2021). Constructing the myth of protest masculinity in Chinese English language news media: A critical discourse analysis of the representation of "leftover men." *Gender and Language*, 15(2), 184–206. https://doi.org/10.1558/genl.18823

Yue, A., and Leung, H. H-S. (2017). Notes towards the queer Asian city: Singapore and Hong Kong. *Urban Studies*, 54(3), 747–764. https://doi.org/10.1177/0042098015602996

Funding Statement

The research in this element was partly funded by the Research Grants Council of the Hong Kong SAR Government and the National Research Council of Thailand (NRCT). We would also like to acknowledge the support of the Center of Excellence in Southeast Asian Linguistics, Chulalongkorn University.

Cambridge Elements

Language, Gender and Sexuality

Helen Sauntson
York St John University

Helen Sauntson is Professor of English Language and Linguistics at York St John University, UK. Her research areas are language in education and language, gender and sexuality. She is co-editor of *The Palgrave Studies in Language, Gender and Sexuality* book series, and she sits on the editorial boards of the journals *Gender and Language* and the *Journal of Language and Sexuality*. Within her institution, Helen is Director of the Centre for Language and Social Justice Research.

Editorial Board
Lilian Lem Atanga, *The University of Bamenda*
Eva Nossem, *Saarland University*
Joshua M. Paiz, *The George Washington University*
M. Agnes Kang, *University of Hong Kong*

About the Series
Cambridge Elements in Language, Gender and Sexuality highlights the role of language in understanding issues, identities and relationships in relation to multiple genders and sexualities. The series provides a comprehensive home for key topics in the field which readers can consult for up-to-date coverage and the latest developments.

Cambridge Elements

Language, Gender and Sexuality

Elements in the Series

The Language of Gender-Based Separatism
Veronika Koller, Alexandra Krendel and Jessica Aiston

Queering Sexual Health Translation Pedagogy
Piero Toto

Legal Categorization of "Transgender": An Analysis of Statutory Interpretation of "Sex", "Man", and "Woman" in Transgender Jurisprudence
Kimberly Tao

LGBTQ+ and Feminist Digital Activism: A Linguistic Perspective
Angela Zottola

Feminism, Corpus-assisted Research and Language Inclusivity
Federica Formato

Queering Language Revitalisation: Navigating Identity and Inclusion among Queer Speakers of Minority Languages
John Walsh, Michael Hornsby, Eva J. Daussà, Renée Pera-Ros, Samuel Parker, Jonathan Morris and Holly R. Cashman

Pride in Asia: Negotiating Ideologies, Localness, and Alternative Futures
Benedict J. L. Rowlett, Pavadee Saisuwan, Christian Go,
Li-Chi Chen and Mie Hiramoto

A full series listing is available at: www.cambridge.org/ELGS